THE EVOLUTION OF MAN

THE WORLD OF SCIENCE LIBRARY
GENERAL EDITOR: ROBIN CLARKE

THE EVOLUTION OF MAN

David Pilbeam

THAMES AND HUDSON · LONDON

To Rosanne,
who helped me far more than she knows

Set by V. Siviter Smith Ltd, Birmingham
Printed in Holland by Smeets Lithographers, Weert
Bound in Holland by Proost en Brandt NV, Amsterdam
500 08003 8 Clothbound
500 10003 9 Paperback

CONTENTS

INTRODUCTION

It is today hardly to be doubted that man is as much a product of the evolutionary process as any other living thing. Knowledge of the particular evidence for human evolution, however, is still not very widely shared. This book accordingly represents a further attempt to convey to the general reader the broad outlines of what is now known about human origins.

I should state at once that it is, in places, a rather personal view, although I hope that I have indicated this in appropriate and obvious ways. The subject is in an extreme state of flux at present, and it is impossible to give a wholly objective account of human evolution, for so much still depends on personal interpretation. Indeed, as I read through the proofs, I anticipate that on publication – some months away yet – there will be a number of points with which I should then be at variance.

Palaeoanthropology – the study of human evolution – is only now coming of age as a science. During the past few years it has emerged from the purely descriptive stage which is the hallmark of a subject's immaturity. Many workers, from studies of skeletal form in relation to function, are attempting to relate functions to behaviour, and therefrom to infer total species behaviour patterns. Evolution is the study of adaptation, and occurs because selective forces change behaviour patterns. What we see in fossils is the result of these changes, and only by inferring past behaviours from the fossil evidence can we talk meaningfully of what happened in evolution, and why.

Man has spent over 99 per cent of the period of his existence on earth as a hunter and gatherer, living in small, widely dispersed groups. This means that most of our basic biology evolved under very different circumstances from those under which we live now. Most of us are urban dwellers, often living in acutely crowded conditions–conditions, it is frequently forgotten, for which we are not biologically 'designed'. Of course, man is a marvellously adaptable creature and can call on a wide variety of 'coping' behaviours to help him in novel surroundings, but his repertoire is not unlimited. I do not wish to imply that palaeoanthropology is going to provide magical answers to our problems. I do believe, though, that only by knowing ourselves thoroughly as animals–albeit immensely clever animals–can we begin to understand why we do things that disturb us, and why we do not always behave to our best advantage. As George Gaylord Simpson remarked, 'One hundred years without Darwin are enough!' It is still true that man behaves the way he does *at least in part* because of his evolutionary history. We do not come into the world as blanks upon which virtually anything can be stamped.

This book is based on a set of introductory lectures given to undergraduates at Cambridge and Yale Universities. I thank all those who helped me to say things better. Many times in going over my notes I discovered places where thoughts were out of sequence, and ideas disorganised or unclear. My apologies go to those who suffered. To the General Editor, Robin Clarke, who suggested that I write this book, go my thanks for his encouragement and expert editorial advice. The manuscript I wrote mostly in Uganda while I was fossil-hunting with Dr. Alan Walker of Nairobi University College. I am grateful to all those on the expedition at that time for providing the perfect atmosphere for writing.

I have not thanked by name all those among my colleagues and students who have helped clarify my ideas, or contributed new ones: I thank them all anyway.

D.R.P.
New Haven,
Connecticut, 1969

EVOLUTION AND MAN

'Descended from the apes! My dear, we will hope that it is not true. But if it is, let us pray that it may not become generally known.' So said the wife of a canon of Worcester Cathedral in 1860, a year during which evolution was very much in the air. That summer, at Oxford, the British Association held its famous meeting during which Huxley, Hooker and other Darwinians debated with their antagonists, among them Samuel Wilberforce, Bishop of Oxford. Wilberforce facetiously asked Huxley during the debate whether he was descended from an ape on his grandmother's side or his grandfather's. Huxley's reply is said to have been:

> If I am asked whether I would choose to be descended from the poor animal of low intelligence and stooping gait, who grins and chatters as we pass, or from a man, endowed with great ability and a splendid position, who should use these gifts to discredit and crush humble seekers after truth, I hesitate what answer to make.

All the fuss came hard on the heels of Charles Darwin's book, *The Origin of Species*, published in 1859. This covered general evolutionary theory, but the human implications are what seem to have upset so many people—including the canon's wife. In 1871 Darwin published another book, *The Descent of Man*, in which he devoted himself exclusively to human evolution. He suggested cautiously that men and the apes

Opposite: an early popular account of the evolution of man—more notable for its ingenuity than its accuracy—published in 1876 by the German naturalist Ernst Haeckel. Above: a caricature of Bishop Samuel Wilberforce, who argued the case against evolution in the great debate of 1860

PUNCH'S ALMANACK FOR 1882.

MAN·IS·BVT·A·WORM·

Darwin himself portrayed in Punch magazine's tongue-in-cheek musing on the implications of evolutionary theory, 1881. Below: the skull cap discovered in the Neander Valley, near Düsseldorf, in 1856: the first skeletal relic of an extinct variety of man to be described scientifically

were most closely related, and that their common ancestor – when found – would have to be called an ape even though it would not, in all probability, resemble any living ape. He wrote:

> It is probable that Africa was formerly inhabited by extinct apes closely allied to the gorilla and chimpanzee; and as these two species are now man's nearest allies, it is somewhat more probable that our early progenitors lived on the African continent than elsewhere.

As regards the region in which the common ancestor would be found, Darwin, in the light of present-day knowledge, was right. As to the ancestor being 'closely allied' to the living African apes, this is still very debatable. When Darwin wrote, he had available almost no fossil primates (the zoological group to which man, apes, monkeys, and certain other more primitive forms belong). Only one extinct ape, *Dryopithecus*, and one extinct man, Neanderthal, were known. Since then many hundreds of pongid (ape or ape-like) and hominid (human or man-like) fossils have been recovered. As a result, the story of man's evolution can now be told, although there are still many points to argue and many gaps to fill in.

The emergence of man

The very earliest primates appear at the end of the period of geological time known as the Cretaceous, and become quite abundant in the succeeding Palaeocene. During this time all primates were simple, small, clawed quadrupeds, scurrying about on all fours, living on the ground and in the trees. In the Eocene, primates finally took to the trees altogether, evolving many novel methods of coping with their new arboreal way of life, in particular by living in social groups, and by relying increasingly on learned rather than on instinctive behaviour. The next epoch, the Oligocene, saw the rise of the so-called higher primates—those most similar to us, the monkeys and apes; they flourished during the Miocene and Pliocene. Some time between the Oligocene and Pliocene, between 35 and 5 million years ago, the pongid and hominid stocks became differentiated. For a long time, perhaps 30 million years or more, the hominids were a rather unimpressive evolutionary line, at least in numbers. But these years saw slow but ultimately enormous changes in behaviour so that by the last geological epoch, the Pleistocene, hominids finally came into their own. Only at this late stage did the human brain expand to its present enormous size.

We humans, who have given ourselves the scientific name of *Homo sapiens*, are a species characterized by a number of anatomical and behavioural features. Most remarkable are our upright posture, our dentition—lacking projecting male canines—and our behaviour; we have carried the extent of our learned behaviour far beyond that found in any other primate. Anthropologists refer to man's extremely complex learned behaviour as 'culture'. Culture embraces all the political, ideological, and technological aspects of society and is

Table of geological epochs since the end of the Cretaceous period, nearly 70 million years ago. The geological history of the earth itself spans more than 4,000 million years; the first living thing probably appeared about 3,000 million years ago; man less than 2 million years ago

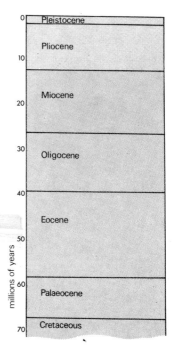

A present-day hunter-gatherer: a bushman of the Kalahari, stalking game

transmitted from generation to generation by teaching and learning rather than by genetic inheritance. There certainly are basic, genetically controlled human behavioural patterns, but those which differ from population to population appear to be due mainly to social differences in learned behaviour. Theodosius Dobzhansky and Ashley Montagu have pointed out that the quality which has been constantly selected throughout human evolution is educability.

Homo sapiens appeared in modern form (there were earlier, more archaic-looking groups of the same species) some 50,000 years ago. Before this, for at least two million years and perhaps ten or more million, humans and human ancestors had hunted and gathered their food. Indeed until only 10,000 years ago all men were still hunter-gatherers, as Pygmies, Bushmen, and Australian Aboriginals are to this day.

Although these non-literate peoples are 'primitive' in a technological sense, in other ways they are emphatically not primitive. Their emotions, human relationships, and languages are no less complex than ours. Victorian travellers' tales of peoples with vocabularies of but a few hundred words, unable to count beyond 5 or 6, tell us more about the gullibility of travellers than about 'primitive' society.

The organization of primitive societies is a reflection of the hunting way of life. The only division of labour is between males and females; thus there is no structuring of society, reflecting economic, political or religious aspects of behaviour. Although there are leaders, these are persons with influence rather than authority, leading by example rather than coercion; the leader will tend to be the most knowledgeable, the most experienced, the most skilled in conciliation. Hunting occurs within a fairly fixed territory, although groups do overlap without quarrelling since adjacent groups will share many kinsfolk as a result of exchanging women–and sometimes men–in marriage. The practice of 'marrying out' (exogamy) is peculiarly human.

There is no private property, only personal property, like knives, bows, cooking utensils. There is a constant

reciprocity in social relationships. The most admired Bushman, for example, is the most generous Bushman. Although feuding and fighting within and between groups does occur, this rarely becomes serious. Wars are impossible; no economic surplus is available to support armies, nor are there surpluses of young men to form armies. Human beings are aggressive, but in primitive society aggression is always channelled and controlled, behaviour being hedged around with customs, rules, and taboos.

Some 10,000 years ago certain human populations in the Near East changed their way of life from that of a hunting community to one based on the domestication of plants and animals. This was the agricultural or so-called Neolithic revolution. With this economic change came the possibility of great increases in population density, together with increased division of labour within a community. The surplus food produced by the farmers could support large numbers of 'non-productive' people, who could become labourers, artisans, soldiers, artists, politicians and scientists. This change in the way of life was enormous, and eventually made possible the achievements of Western science-based civilization. It should be emphasized however that the change was wholly cultural; it took place far too quickly and too recently to be associated with biological changes in individuals.

Early evidence of human settlement: a representation of a large village at the foot of a volcano, painted by an Anatolian artist, at Çatal Hüyük in the Near East, about 8,000 years ago. Below: an 11,000-year-old formal burial of a Natufian chieftain, in Syria. The skull, carefully propped up with stones, faces Mount Hermon

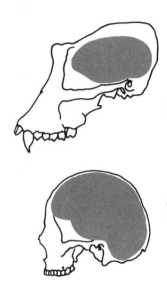

Above: the relative sizes of the brains of the gorilla (top) and man, viewed laterally. Opposite: vertical aspects

Culture in all its complexities is a direct product of the human brain. Man's brain is three times as large as that of the chimpanzee or the gorilla, the most intelligent non-human primates. Not only is it larger, but it is organized differently. It appears almost certain that the intricate structure of the human brain is specially adapted above all to the learning of language in such a way as to generate simple rules of construction or grammar. Human dwarfs with brains no bigger than chimpanzee brains, and with fewer brain cells, are capable of acquiring language. Many people assume that we have big brains in order to be 'clever' and 'intelligent' in a Western sense – to cogitate, to manipulate facts, to reason. More probably the brain became increasingly large and complex in response to the superior capacity to survive afforded by its ability to master language and grasp social rules with increasing rapidity during early childhood, and by its ability to act as a kind of filter, removing uninformative, and even misinformative 'noise' from a complex social environment.

The appearance of a brain capable of language, and therefore human, was perhaps the most dramatic of all evolutionary developments. Language enables us not only to describe our private thoughts and motives, but also to refer to external objects and to attach verbal symbols to abstracts which would otherwise remain 'internal'. Only when the categories 'mother', 'father', 'son', 'daughter' and so on can be named is it possible to have incest taboos. By 'incest taboos' anthropologists mean the whole set of sexual relationships between relatives which are more or less universally forbidden in human society. It is now becoming apparent that in many primates matings between some close relatives do not occur, or do so only very infrequently; but this is because of differences in their behaviour patterns. Only language enables the relatives, and their relationships, to be named, categorized and the behaviour patterns to be elevated to the status of a universal code of behaviour. Indeed the same can be said for all human ethical behaviour. Naming reinforces behaviour patterns, some of which may already have been present before the origin of language.

Man's hominid ancestry

By the term 'human' anthropologists mean creatures similar enough to ourselves to warrant being classified in the same group or genus – *Homo*. Yet membership of the genus *Homo* is to a very large extent determined arbitrarily because our definitions can be altered to suit ourselves. Membership is arbitrary for another reason too. If we accept the idea of human evolution, obviously we have ancestors who did not look exactly like us. And the farther back in time we go, the less they will resemble us. As we discover more and more fossils and fill in the gaps in the record, our fossil history will increasingly appear as a continuum, until finally it will be impossible to draw any clear-cut line distinguishing human from non-human fossils.

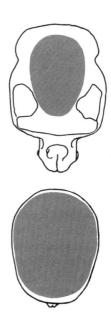

Our ancestors in the late Pleistocene, between 200,000 and 50,000 years ago, were large-brained like us and perfectly upright too, but differed in that their skulls were long and low. A rather extreme example of these types were the Neanderthals of Western Europe. True Neanderthals were probably not ancestral to any living men, although our ancestors would not have differed greatly from them. These ancestors are grouped with us in *Homo sapiens*, a way of saying that the differences between us and them are less important than the similarities.

Men of the middle Pleistocene, from one to half a million years ago, differed still more. Although they were fully upright, their brains were only two-thirds the size of ours, and they were almost certainly less clever than us. These hominids are considered human enough to be placed in the genus *Homo*, but different enough to warrant another species name, *Homo erectus.*

The species boundary between *H. erectus* and *H. sapiens* is generally and arbitrarily drawn between 500,000 and 300,000 years ago. It is important to appreciate that this 'boundary' did not in fact exist. *H. erectus* did not hurdle it to become *H. sapiens*! We are simply

chopping up a continuum for our own convenience so that we can compare different parts of it. We might otherwise end by calling amoebae *H. sapiens*.

Hominids of the early Pleistocene, two to one million years ago, are deemed different enough from the genus *Homo* to be given a completely new generic name, *Australopithecus.* There are several kinds of *Australopithecus*, but mostly they were small pygmy-sized creatures who nevertheless moved as we do, and had human-type teeth, but relatively tiny ape-sized brains. Before the Pleistocene the fossil record is scanty, but there is some evidence which suggests that hominids

Some key stages in the evolution of man, reconstructed from fossil remains. Left to right: Dryopithecus (Proconsul), an ape living some 20 million years ago, thought to resemble the common ancestor of apes and men; Australopithecus, who flourished about 2 million years ago and was probably the first toolmaker; Pekin man (an example of Homo erectus), whose remains are about half a million years old; Neanderthal man, who occupied Europe for much of the last 100,000 years; Mount Carmel man, who lived 40–45,000 years ago, an early example of Homo sapiens; and Cro-Magnon man, anatomically indistinguishable from man today

and pongids separated at least 14 million years ago.
Throughout much of the pre-Pleistocene time, particularly in the Pliocene, hominids may have been tool-users. This type of behaviour is unusual for primates, or indeed for any animal. In the early Pleistocene deliberately-shaped stone tools are found in deposits with the hominids, showing that the latter were tool-makers; tool-making became more sophisticated as brains grew larger during the Pleistocene. To trace this story properly, however, we must look to the fossils themselves, and let them show the strengths and inadequacies of what we know about our pre-history.

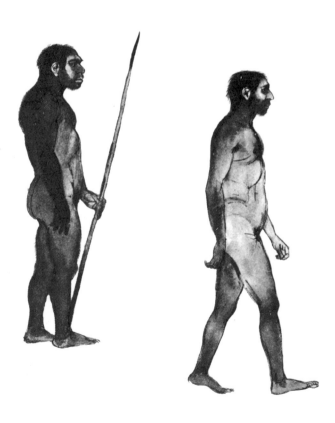

THE SUBSTANCE OF EVOLUTION **2**

Animals do not exist in a vacuum; they inhabit and interact with an environment that includes animals of their own and other species as well as plants. Primates are clever; for the most part they are among the cleverest of all living animals and their interactions with their total environment are complex in the extreme. It is the animal's behaviour which, so to speak, connects it to the environment, and, through behaviour, the environment moulds the final structure of the individual.

Examine, for example, the human foot, and compare it to the same organ in an ape. (The human structure is probably derived from something more or less like the ape's foot.) The ape is built to be most efficiently a quadrupedal, climbing form. Man on the other hand shows many adaptations to *upright* walking and running on the ground. Note the set of the big toe in man, parallel to the other shorter toes; also the arch system of the foot, to cope with weight transmission. All these features are correlated with a particular type of locomotion–habitual upright bipedalism. Now, unless millions of individual human ancestors had been walking and running around (that is to say, behaving as upright bipeds), these and other parts of the skeleton involved in walking would never have become structurally so well adapted.

How this adaptation came about was first explained by Darwin with his theory of natural selection. During

Opposite: the patriarchal figure of Charles Darwin (1809–82) towards the end of his life, on the verandah of his home, Down House, in Sussex. Below: foot skeletons of the gorilla (top) and man, each adapted to a special mode of locomotion

The variety of finch species peculiar to the Galapagos Islands provided Darwin with an important clue to the origin of species. Above: differences in bill size evident in some of the finches

The woodpecker finch, remarkable for its habitual use of a twig to dislodge insects, photographed on the Galapagos by I. Eibl-Eibesfeldt

the voyage of the *Beagle* in the 1830s Darwin, who was ship's naturalist, became convinced that evolution had in fact occurred. During this cruise he began to observe animals and their variations and not merely to kill and preserve them for display in museum collections.

The portion of the voyage which impressed him most was his study of the birds of the Galapagos Islands off the Pacific Coast of South America. He assumed that the islands had originally been colonized from the South American mainland by only a very small number of bird species – particularly by some finches. He concluded that the latter, presumably of a single species, had with time become greatly diversified on the various islands and had produced there more than a dozen species, far more than their mainland relatives. Individual species had evolved many features commonly seen in rather different types of birds (that is, in non-finches), and had evolved structures and behaviours that were appropriate to their new situations. The original finches had split up into new species each of which had colonized a new 'ecological niche' – its own little piece of the environment. Some had developed beaks like woodpeckers, others beaks like warblers, yet clearly they were still basically finches.

Darwin began to write *The Origin of Species* in 1837, but did not publish it until 1859. Two years after starting to write it he read Malthus's *Essay on Population*, which finally suggested to him the mechanism of evolution. Malthus's theory on population growth was simple. Population tends to expand at a steadily increasing rate, while food supply only grows at a constant rate. Population is therefore bound to outrun food supply, and unless there are checks on population increases, excess population will die of starvation. This suggested to Darwin his theory of natural selection. Like all good scientific theories it has the great advantage of elegance and simplicity; it also explains evolution. The theory may be summarized as follows:

All animal species naturally vary, individual by individual, whatever trait or traits are considered. The variation which occurs is at least in part genetically

determined. Nowadays it is recognized that it is an oversimplification to divide characters into two categories—those that are genetically determined, and those that are moulded by the environment during an individual's growth. Rather, every feature is seen as resulting from the interaction during growth and development of both genetic and environmental factors.

Considering this natural variability within a species, some animals are better equipped, or *adapted*, to cope with their environment and to survive than are other animals. Those traits which determine whether or not an animal is able to survive and reproduce are more or less controlled by that individual's genetic inheritance (genotype), and this inheritance is passed on to any offspring.

Not all offspring survive to reproduce themselves. Those individuals which are less well adapted tend not to reproduce, and thus the genetic factors responsible

Mammals well adapted to an aquatic environment: a dolphin cow and her newborn calf

for poor adaptation tend to be weeded out. Gradually, over thousands of years, a population's collection of genetic determinants alters and hence the average anatomy, physiology, and behaviour of the population alters too. The better adapted individuals leave behind more offspring than the less well adapted; the better adapted therefore increase in number. Evolution is occurring.

The first, and perhaps the most important point to be made about the theory of natural selection is that the environment acts as a selecting agent, as a sieve, rather than as an electing agent. The environment merely determines whether or not an individual reproduces, and with what success. The second and related point is that individuals themselves do not evolve, only populations. The post-Darwinian, Victorian view of natural selection was of vicious competition between individuals and species—'nature red in tooth and claw'—a view, incidentally, never adopted by Darwin himself. The truth of the matter, however, is rather more subtle. Animals do not continually go around fighting each other; rather, the success which really counts is repro-

Failure to preadapt to changing environmental conditions led ultimately to the extinction of the dinosaurs. Below: the skeleton of an Iguanodon, a dinosaur which stood 16 feet high

ductive success. Those animals that leave relatively more offspring than others are 'fitter' or more successful. The 'fittest' animals are not necessarily the biggest, strongest, fastest, or sexually most attractive; merely those that leave the most progeny. It is interesting to find that approximately half the human females of one generation produce over three-quarters of the next generation—a ratio which seems to apply equally to Australian Aboriginals and Western Europeans.

We have, then, a picture of evolution as constant and quite subtle genetic changes from one generation to another. It is just possible to show a few of these changes actually occurring in living species, although doing this is obviously difficult, for it is usually only over a large number of generations that biochemical or detectable structural changes become apparent. After all, this is what most of us picture by the term 'evolution'—detectable change in a sequence of related forms extended through time.

The key concept is 'adaptation'. Adaptation is what happens as, with the passage of generations, a species gradually becomes better able to survive in its environment. It is the outcome of natural selection: constant adjustments result as the environment weeds out the less fit, thereby improving the adaptation of the species as a whole to its specific pressures. Of course, it may happen that the environment itself changes, and possibly with a rapidity to which the species cannot adapt. A well adapted species may thus become ill adapted to survive.

The converse is also possible and leads to the idea of 'preadaptation'. A species is said to be preadapted if it is able to shift successfully from its old habitat into a new one—if it can colonize a new environmental niche. A structure or a behavioural pattern is preadapted if it can assume a new function in a new context without interfering with the original function. The concept of preadaptation helps us to understand how radical innovations in behaviour can appear during evolution. Of course, preadaptation is only a convenient way of thinking about evolutionary events; there is nothing purposive about the characteristics that are labelled as preadaptations.

The definition of species

Among primates, as in other sexually reproducing animals, species consist of individuals bound together by actual or potential reproductive relationships. All living men belong to a single species, *Homo sapiens*. All living chimpanzees belong to another, *Pan troglodytes*; and gorillas to *Gorilla gorilla*. Gorillas do not interbreed with chimpanzees, nor with men. The species are kept distinct by the fact that they do not interbreed, and therefore never exchange genetic material. Species are defined as the largest natural groups of animals that are actually (or potentially) capable of interbreeding with the production of fully fertile offspring.

There are, however, also many examples of species crossing and producing viable offspring. Donkeys crossed with horses yield mules; most of these are sterile, although about one in a thousand is not. Under experimental conditions species of baboons and macaques can be paired and will produce offspring which are apparently fully fertile with either parental group. The

A 'Zebrorse' with marked zebra stripes, produced by the mating of a zebra stallion with a horse mare: living proof that the crossing of different species is not necessarily impossible

crosses do not occur in the wild, because the species would never normally meet. Hence the word 'natural' in the species definition, meaning 'in the natural environment'. Some species of baboon live in adjacent geographical areas; in the contact zone, they hybridize. But this zone remains narrow, suggesting that hybrids are relatively less fit. (If this were not so, the two species would not be distinct for long.) Very occasionally, in the wild, a primate of one species may join up with a troop of another species, and may even mate within the other troop. These are always very rare occurrences, though, and probably have next to no influence on the evolutionary future of either species.

Some would argue that these exceptions render useless all attempts to define species. Species, however, not only tend to evolve through time, changing their 'average' genetic make-up; they also multiply, splitting mother species into two or more daughter species. This process of splitting is termed 'speciation' and generally occurs when part of the population is isolated by some geographical barrier; the isolated population evolves, changes occurring in genetic make-up, in structure and appearance (morphology), and in characteristic be- haviour patterns of successive generations of individuals in response to the new environment; so that later when there may be a renewed opportunity for back-crossing with the original species, mating barriers have developed that prevent or limit hybridization.

Now, if speciation is complete, and if genetic change has proceeded far enough, no hybridization at all will be possible. If, however, speciation is not quite complete, or if the new species is not genetically very different from the old, some crossing will still be possible. This is merely what we should expect from the evolutionary theory. Yet, once again, although genetic material can be exchanged between species, such exchange is unimportant in an evolutionary sense to either species. If it were important, the two would cease to be species.

Because morphology is quite closely related to an individual's genetic make-up, and because individuals within a species have more or less similar genetic make-ups, species contain individuals which resemble one another more or less. All will differ from members of other species. It is most important to remember that individuals are similar because they belong in the same species, not vice versa. We can use this similarity of individuals to define species on purely morphological grounds, including under each species those individuals that are sufficiently similar to one another. Obviously, this is the only way in which we can sort fossils into species. Species defined in this way are called morpho-species, as opposed to the genetically defined species we have been discussing.

Palaeontologists sort their fossils into a particular type of morphospecies called evolutionary or time-successive species. These are lineages extending through time. At all stages the lineages are circumscribed, so to speak, by reproductive boundaries. Species within such lineages do not, indeed cannot, have a definite beginning or end. The boundaries between successive evolutionary species are arbitrary and are made for our own descriptive convenience. The boundaries are completely different from those which separate, say, living man and gorillas.

The classification of species

Classification – the process of grouping individuals into more inclusive categories – starts with species, the units which evolve. The arrangement of species into higher groups, and the naming in turn of these groups are rather more arbitrary steps. Early zoologists classified species in order to reflect what they saw as the order inherent in creation. Nowadays, similar species are grouped together because classification specialists (taxonomists) believe that their similarity is due to recent shared ancestry; the more closely similar the species, the closer the time of branching.

Species are given two italicized Latin names – for example, *Homo sapiens*, our own species. An earlier species of man, more primitive than ourselves, has been classified as *Homo erectus*. *Homo* is the generic name (or genus name) and *H. sapiens* and *H. erectus* are considered similar enough to be placed in the same genus. They are time-successive species. Similar groupings are found among living animals. The dog, *Canis familiaris*, and the wolf, *Canis lupus*, are placed in the same genus, in this instance because they share a very recent common ancestor and have changed relatively little since the time of that ancestor.

When originally discovered, the middle Pleistocene hominid *H. erectus* was described as *Pithecanthropus erectus*. Nowadays, if such a generic name were used for a fossil hominid, this would be taken to imply that this species was at least as different from *H. sapiens* as lion, *Panthera leo*, differs from wild cat, *Felis sylvestris*. However, it is clear that this is not the case with *Pithecanthropus erectus* so it has been transferred by most anthropologists to *Homo*. The species name *erectus* is still retained, but *Pithecanthropus* is dropped because *Homo* was the name used first. Although most anthropologists preferred to call *Pithecanthropus* by the name *Homo*, transferring a fossil species from one genus to another is a matter of opinion; there are obviously no interbreeding criteria which can be applied. So although taxonomists may follow the same rules, their opinions can and do vary and change, just like those of lawyers.

All species have to have a type specimen in order to be 'valid'. This should not be confused with a typical or average specimen, but rather it is the one specimen, in some collection, to which the species name was originally applied. The type does not change, but the limits of the species often do with the discovery of additional material.

Clearly, when we classify living or extinct animals on the basis of similarities, we want to be sure that their similarities are of the right sort. We want to choose structures that have a similar genetic basis. Bats and insects would not be classified together just because both have wings. Bats are mammals and related to other mammals like ourselves, who use fore-limbs for holding objects, and also to whales, whose fore-limbs are modified into fins. Insects on the other hand are invertebrates and more closely related to molluscs and annelids than they are to bats. So we would not choose wings as a useful character in this particular case, because the structures are similar only in that they have the same function. They are called 'analogous' structures. Suppose, on the other hand, we take a human foot, and compare it to a gorilla foot. Although different, the two are nevertheless basically similar. They share the same bony elements–tarsals, metatarsals and phalanges; although any given bone will vary in shape and size between the species, all are simply variations on the same theme, reflecting slight genetic differences. In this case, the similarities are due to 'homology', the two feet being 'homologues'. Homology is similarity due to descent from a common ancestor. In constructing classifications, and in reconstructing evolutionary histories, it is essential to be able to recognize homologues. In this way we should be able to produce good approximations to the true scheme of evolutionary events, and also classifications with the greatest information content.

But is there not an element of circular reasoning in all this? We use homologies to group species together, and to construct evolutionary lineages. We then turn round and say that the similarities we are using must be homologies because of the evolutionary relationships between the species involved! We can break the ring of apparent circularity by accepting that, given close and detailed enough similarity, it is the most reasonable hypothesis to believe that similarities are indeed homologies. It is the most plausible explanation. To state, for example, that *Homo erectus* is ancestral to *Homo sapiens*, is really to say that because of the many widespread and detailed similarities between the two it is safe to argue that one is descended from the other. Of course, *H. erectus* may not be a hominid at all; it might be a man-like ape, or monkey, or even a man-like horse! The latter alternative may be preposterous, but all we have done is to list the various alternatives in descending order of probability. The most probable is that *H. erectus* is indeed a hominid.

The wings of the bat, barn owl and dragonfly (opposite) are 'analogues' in that they all have the same function. Since the wings of the bat (a mammal) and the bird are, unlike those of the insect, modifications of the same basic vertebrate forelimbs, they are also homologues. Insect wings are the result of an entirely separate evolutionary development

KINGDOM:	Animalia
PHYLUM:	Chordata
CLASS:	Mammalia
ORDER:	Primates
FAMILY:	Hominidae
GENUS:	*Homo*
SPECIES:	*Homo sapiens*

Some of the main biological categories to which modern man, Homo sapiens, belongs

So genera will, we hope, include species which tend to have shared a most recent common ancestor. Within genera species are sometimes packaged into subgenera. Subgeneric names are placed in parentheses after the generic name. Similar genera are grouped in subfamilies, and subfamilies into families. More inclusive still are superfamilies and we continue up through infraorders and suborders to orders. The Primates are but one of the orders of the class Mammalia. All these levels of classification contain sets which can be described as taxa. Thus the species *H. sapiens* is a taxon, and the order Primates is too. Living and extinct men and their ancestors are placed in the family Hominidae (standard family ending: '-idae'). Apes are classified in the Pongidae. Living apes are termed Ponginae (standard subfamily ending: '-inae'), while extinct species are grouped in the Dryopithecinae, named after the Tertiary pongid *Dryopithecus*. The gibbons (*Hylobates*) and siamangs, or lesser apes, are distantly related both to Pongidae and Hominidae; they are placed in the family Hylobatidae. All three families are clustered in the Hominoidea (superfamily ending: '-oidea'). When colloquial terms are used they must be applied properly. Thus 'hominids' are members of the family Hominidae, 'pongids' of the Pongidae, 'pongines' of the Ponginae, and so on.

As far as possible, classifications above the species level are used to reflect the evolutionary history of the groups within them. Thus, gibbons, great apes, and men seem (from the evidence of the fossil record and the anatomy and genetics of the living species) to be about equally related in terms of common ancestry. They are therefore given coordinate status in three families. (Some workers, however, believe that gibbons are really just little pongids, and only make them a subfamily within the Pongidae.) Although the aim of classification is to reflect evolutionary relationships, this is always a difficult thing to reach agreement upon because evolution consists not only of branching but of change within a lineage as well. This latter type of change can occur at different rates; thus, early hominoids might have split into two groups, one ancestral to gorillas, the other ancestral both to chimpanzees and men. In this sense men and chimps are more closely 'related' to each other than to gorillas. But hominids have clearly diverged far more from chimpanzees than chimps have from gorillas. It would be meaningless to classify men and chimpanzees in one group, with gorillas in another. One is forced to compromise.

Before we turn to the primates in detail, two more useful terms should be noted. These are 'primitive' and 'specialized' (or 'advanced'). These terms sometimes seem to express an author's opinions as to the success or failure of a group and are not always based strictly on biological criteria. They should therefore be defined and used precisely. First, 'primitive' and 'specialized' are meaningless unless applied within a lineage; earlier characters are 'primitive', later ones 'advanced'. Thus, early hominids with large teeth are more primitive in this character than later ones with smaller teeth. Second, in a given group, characters resembling the common ancestor are primitive. So, within Hominoidea, ape feet are more primitive than ours.

Three members of the superfamily Hominoidea (to which man himself belongs), a chimpanzee, a gibbon and an orang utan, in a setting intended to stress their human affinities

THE PRIMATES

The order Primates contains species which are more or less primitive living alongside those showing varying degrees of specialization. This is most helpful to the anthropologist for it enables him, by using extant forms as models, to reconstruct with some confidence fossil morphology and functional anatomy–particularly useful in the study of locomotor evolution. Moreover, there is the possibility that the behaviour of primate species today may provide insights into the early evolution of human behaviour.

Primates are classified into two basic subdivisions or suborders: Prosimii (so-called lower primates), and Anthropoidea (higher primates–monkeys, apes, and men). The subdivisions reflect certain fundamental facts of anatomy, behaviour and evolutionary history. Prosimians are generally small, primitive animals with relatively smaller brains than those of the other primates. They are less intelligent in the sense that their manipulative behaviour and ability to cope with unusual or novel situations is not so highly developed as in the Anthropoidea. But they are built basically like other primates, and it is possible to see in them a pre-higher-primate level of development.

All non-human primates show evidence of being adapted to an arboreal way of life. Even the species which are to a considerable extent ground-dwellers still sleep and take refuge in trees. The original primate

Probably the best known of all primates other than man himself is the chimpanzee (Pan troglodytes), a native of the forests of central Africa. Opposite: the pensive face of a young male

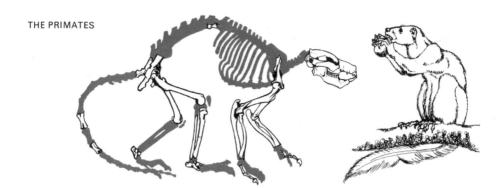

An example of an early primate from the Palaeocene: Plesiadapis, reconstructed from French and North American fossil finds (unshaded). It died out more than 50 million years ago

adaptation was to tree living, a way of life avoiding most of the ever-present predators.

Teeth are the body parts most frequently preserved as fossils because of their hard enamel coat. Each species has a distinctive set of tooth features, and this enables palaeontologists to sort the fossils into species and lineages, working from their preserved teeth; with the inclusion of evidence from skulls and limb bones, as they are available, a good picture emerges.

Early primates and modern prosimians

Primates first appeared in the fossil record about 70 million years ago, although during the Cretaceous they are known only from their teeth. They are all very primitive during the Palaeocene, and those whose skeletons are known from that time were clawed quadrupeds looking rather like rats. Most of these primates became extinct without issue, but some lived on into the Eocene. The Eocene saw a tremendous flowering of the primates. Large numbers are known, in great diversity, from North America, Europe, and Asia and it is possible that they lived in Africa and South America too, although so far no deposits of Eocene age in these areas have yielded primates. Eocene primates were the first to evolve the particular arboreal adaptations so typical of later primates. (The first true rodents also appear in the Eocene, and it is thought likely that the evolution of these very successful mammals nudged the primates into becoming highly adapted to exlusively arboreal niches.) The primates of the Eocene had larger brains than their ancestors, and relatively larger brains than almost all other mammals. Their large eyes were directed forward rather than sideways, giving overlapping fields of vision, and their faces were becoming shorter as snouts became smaller with the reduced importance of the sense of smell. All these changes are correlated with the adoption of tree-living as a way of life. Primates live in a three-dimensional world, one where accurate vision for judging distance is vitally important, and where the sense of smell is not.

These early primates had one other major adaptation, climbing by grasping. Instead of having to dig claws into bark, they were able to grasp branches with thumb and great toe behind, and fingers and toes in front. Primates retained the primitive mammalian five-digit hand, but set the thumb and great toe apart from the others so that hands and feet could be used like pincers. Nails replaced claws to support the sensitive pulp pads at the ends of digits. A whole set of related adaptations are also found. The wrist, elbow, and shoulder joints are very mobile; the two forearm bones can be rotated round each other; the hip joint also permits considerable mobility. These features make climbing by grasping that much easier.

The Eocene prosimians all seem to have had one basic locomotor adaptation. They were no longer quadrupeds, but vertical clingers and leapers. Vertical clinging and leaping is an extremely important locomotor category, perhaps originally evolved as an effective means of avoiding predators. It is an arboreal mode of progressing in which the hind limbs only are used for locomotion. The trunk is vertical before and after each leap as well as in the resting position, during which the animal prefers vertical supports too. On those rare occasions when they do come to the ground, vertical clingers and leapers indulge in bipedal hopping and walking, with the trunk held upright. There are many skeletal adaptations to this type of leaping, and these can be seen in early Prosimians.

Living prosimians are not unlike these Eocene primates; from a study of today's animals we can infer much about the habits of the extinct ones. The nocturnal forms were probably solitary, but diurnal species would have lived in social groups. Primate social groupings are unusual among mammals in that adult males and females, together with infants, are associated in more or less permanent societies. For many years it was assumed that this type of society was only possible for the more intelligent higher primates, but recent field work on Malagasy prosimians has shown that permanent societies probably evolved before the highly developed intelligence and manipulative skills so typical of higher primates.

There are many advantages to living in social groups. Group protection is one. Because the young can grow within the protection of the troop they are able to mature more slowly and to spend more time learning the skills necessary for later survival. As learned behaviour becomes a more and more important part of total behaviour, this total behaviour grows increasingly complex. As complexity increases the flexibility of response to particular situations also increases, to the clear benefit of the species. Obviously, many aspects of behaviour are innate, or genetically determined – panting, shivering, and so forth – but it becomes impractical to have all behaviour genetically determined and thus without flexibility, and to have to wait for natural selection to act before behaviour can be changed. Learning provides a self-correcting mechanism which acts very quickly, within the life span of individuals. The adaptiveness of all this is obvious. One animal exposed to a dangerous situation can communicate the awareness of danger to other animals. Infants learn to avoid or deal with danger without ever themselves being exposed to it.

Once it was thought that animals could be divided into two categories: men (who were intelligent and had learned behaviour) and other animals (who were governed by instinct). Actual studies of species in zoos, laboratories, and their natural environments show that

Prosimians of Madagascar. Opposite top: three lemurs in captivity. Bottom: ring-tailed lemurs (Lemur catta) in a forest glade. Above: largest of prosimians, the indris

A tarsier

A pair of galagos or bush-babies

nothing could be further from the truth. Mammals as a group are very intelligent, and none more so than the primates. Societies and behaviour patterns of monkeys and apes are almost unbelievably more complicated than was once thought. Clearly, human sociability and intelligence have origins rooted deep in our pre-human ancestry.

The living prosimians all live in marginal areas (islands like Madagascar) or niches. Those living on the African and Asian continents are nocturnal animals, thus avoiding both diurnal predators and competition from diurnal higher primates. The tarsiers of Southeast Asia and the galagos, or bush-babies, of Africa are small insectivorous vertical clingers and leapers; some

species of *Galago* are somewhat quadrupedal too. Tarsiers are probably descendants of a group of Eocene Prosimii, the Necrolemuridae, known so far only from European deposits. The galagos are widely distributed in Africa. Their ancestors are known from Miocene deposits in East Africa of about 20 million years ago, and at this time they were already very similar to living species of *Galago*. Closely related to the galagos are the lorises, four species of which are divided equally between Africa and Asia. The lorises are arboreal slow-climbing quadrupeds which move with great deliberation. Many features indicate that they have evolved from the bush-babies, probably within the past 25 million years. They are forest-living animals, and almost certainly originated in Africa, migrating thence to Asia. This implies the existence of a forested link between the two continents, probably during the early Miocene (25 to 20 million years ago), for the lorises are highly arboreal creatures.

A third group of surviving prosimians is found in Madagascar and has been isolated there for perhaps 35 million years or more. They have been remarkably lucky for the island has relatively few rodents and carnivores and no higher primates as competition. These primates can be divided into two basic groups, Lemuridae and Indriidae. Living lemurids are almost all quadrupedal, while the indriids are vertical clingers and leapers. Although most workers have regarded the lemurids of genus *Lemur* as the typical prosimians, this is not the case since the 'typical' form would be a vertical clinger. The diurnal lemurids (some others are nocturnal) are gregarious quadrupeds living in small social groups. One species, *Lemur catta*, is of great interest because in both behaviour and anatomy (after all, one reflects the other) it is an intermediate between vertical clingers and leapers on the one hand, and quadrupeds on the other. The quadrupedal lemurs have longer arms than vertical clingers and leapers and use all four limbs in running and leaping. Quadrupedal forms presumably evolved because of slight alterations in niches.

Slender lorises. A mother and her offspring

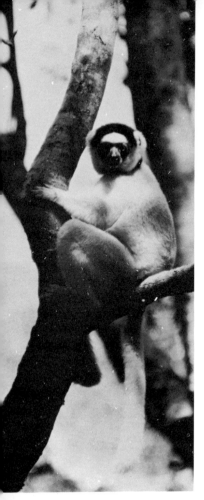

Propithecus. Like the indris, a vertical clinger and leaper

The indriids are vertical clingers and leapers. Two living genera, *Indri* and *Propithecus*, are quite large animals–the largest living prosimians. They are diurnal, and live in small social groups. Until about a thousand years ago, indriids were much more diverse than they are today. With the invasion of the island by man, many species became extinct. Several of these species were rather extraordinary, and, because of the elegant work of Dr Alan Walker, their locomotor behaviour is now understood in detail. Some species were large vertical clingers and leapers. Others were quadrupeds, but quadrupeds showing numerous adaptations to ground living: changes in the hands, feet, and limbs for speedier running, and in the jaws and teeth as adaptations to a diet of grass and roots. They probably became ground–dwellers during the Pliocene (within the past 10 million years) when grassland replaced forest in many parts of the world. They are very similar in their locomotor adaptations to the ground-living African monkeys. Perhaps the most extraordinary of all the extinct lemurs is *Palaeopropithecus*. This species had arms almost half as long again as legs. Hands and feet were great curved hooks, obviously used for hanging and grasping. Shoulder, elbow, wrist, hip, and ankle joints were all adapted for mobility rather than stability. We are dealing here with a rather peculiar animal, one that was capable of suspending itself by the arms below supports and of progressing by arm-swinging using the arms alone. Such locomotion is termed 'brachiation'. The legs and feet were used too in this case and perhaps it would be best to describe the animal as 'quadrumanous', since it used all four extremities. Just as the change from vertical clinger and leaper to quadruped was due to subtle changes in behaviour, diet and ecological niche (the place and role of a species within an environmental complex), so it was with the change to brachiation. Actually, this term does not describe the locomotion of an animal as well as does quadrupedalism, for a brachiator inevitably uses its hind limbs a great deal of the time. Brachiation is perhaps better viewed as a particular feeding adaptation which enables the animal to move out into the smaller branches of trees by grasping handfuls and footfuls of small branches. Thicker supports are not required. Arm and leg mobility means that brachiators can reach in all directions.

We can draw important conclusions from the locomotor study of all prosimians, living and extinct, and from Malagasy species in particular. The earliest prosimians were vertical clingers and leapers, as are many of the living species. This we can regard as a hind-limb dominated type of locomotion. Many prosimians have evolved out of this stage and have become arboreal quadrupeds; *Lemur catta* is a good example of a species intermediate between the two broad classes. Quadrupedalism is a locomotor stage in which arms and legs are of more or less equal length and importance, although legs are still used actively in leaping and are still relatively long compared to trunk length. Finally, arms can become longer still and be used to suspend the body during feeding, and also to move the body by arm-swinging or brachiation. This can be termed a fore-limb dominated locomotor pattern. We can sum up the general trend of prosimian locomotor evolution as a series of shifts from hind-limb dominated to fore-limb dominated locomotor patterns. Obviously, these changes would form a continuum, and the terms 'vertical clinging and leaping', 'quadrupedalism', and 'brachiation' impose quite arbitrary categories within this continuum. Nevertheless, they are useful terms, particularly for the palaeontologist.

As we shall see, the higher primates are all quadrupeds or brachiators, and in all lineages of the Anthropoidea the trend seems to have been towards ever more fore-limb dominated types of locomotion. This trend occurs independently in unrelated lineages; in both lower and higher primates, animals of different groups can develop remarkable similarities in many parts of their skeleton. These changes are good examples of parallel evolution – the evolution in two or more groups of similar adaptations due to similar selective pressures. The selective pressures are acting on animals which are actually rather closely related, and so they are acting on genetic make-ups that are not too dissimilar. The similarities are thus homologues. Parallelism has been far more widespread in primate evolution, at all levels of classification, than was once supposed.

Prosimians can teach us lessons other than those having to do with locomotion. The diurnal Malagasy prosimians have, given their unique chance, evolved social groupings just like higher primates. Their behaviour has been studied by Dr Alison Jolly and the following is drawn mainly from her research. The importance of social groupings has already been noted, and the way in which learned behaviour plays an ever greater part in life in a social context. There are other changes in behaviour too. Adults actively seek body contact with others, and like to play with infants. This behaviour can be interpreted as a carry-over into adult life of behaviour which was once typical just of mother/infant and inter-infant relationships. Mutual grooming is also important, and both body contact and grooming act as a kind of social cement, maintaining group cohesion. Prosimians groom each other using their front teeth, almost all species having specially modified lower canines and incisors forming a projecting dental comb. (Higher primates groom using their hands.) Play behaviour in the young is elaborate and enables infants to develop the locomotor and manipulative skills that are useful in later life. It also enables them to 'learn their place' within the troop. The dominance relationships of later life are first worked out in the pre-adult phases. Dominance itself is a rather diffuse concept, but it is said that one animal is dominant in relation to another if it has preferential access to food, sleeping position, or desired area, mates, and so on, and also if it consistently wins fights. Relative dominance within a troop may change from one behaviour category to the next. In higher primates, dominance relationships are complex in the extreme. In *Lemur catta*, females are dominant to males, the only primate for which this is the case. In this species the breeding season spans only two weeks of each year, and indi-

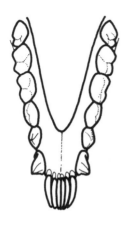

Lemur lower jaw, showing the projecting dental 'comb', well suited to grooming activities

vidual females may only be receptive for a day or so of that. This is a very peculiar arrangement, but it does suggest that it is not primate sexuality alone (or even mainly) that holds the troop together.

In many mammals, aggression is a dispersing mechanism. In order to stay together social mammals need to reduce innate aggression, and also to evolve elaborate sets of checks and balances by developing postures, gestures, and vocalizations which convey information about an animal's emotional state so that others of the group can take appropriate action. Group cohesion, on the other hand, is actively promoted by grooming, play, sexual behaviour and so forth.

Prosimians are clever enough to make their rather complex social organizations work. Learning abilities on the part of individuals have to increase as the social structure becomes increasingly complex; the young

Ring-tailed lemur and young. This species is unique among primates in that the female is dominant to the male

43

are thus afforded more protection and can mature more slowly. With slower maturation, more learning is possible, and so there is a spiral interaction between social dependence and intelligence.

In general, however, prosimians are not very clever with objects. They are not much good at laboratory tests nor are they up to coping with too many unusual events in their natural habitat. The higher primates are better at manipulating objects, have better visual discrimination of the environment, and are generally much cleverer than prosimians. Yet typically primate social groups–adult males and females together with infants in more or less stable troops–evolved before the development of this intelligence. The prosimian stage is therefore preadaptive in many poorly-understood and subtle ways.

The rise of monkeys

During the period between 45 and 35 million years ago (during the Eocene and Oligocene) certain groups of primates, the Anthropoidea, evolved from the prosimian level to a new 'grade' of organization. Wholly novel types appeared, to live side by side with the declining prosimians. The boundary was crossed by several groups of animals; it can be recognized by changes in brain size and structure, in skull form, in the dentition, in locomotor behaviour, and–as far as can be inferred–in social behaviour, diet, and ecology. The Anthropoidea or higher primates are divided into two basic divisions, Platyrrhini (New World monkeys) and Catarrhini (Old World monkeys, apes, and men). The catarrhines are further subdivided into two superfamilies: the monkeys, Cercopithecoidea, and apes and men, Hominoidea. These superfamilies are rather more closely related to each other than either is to the New World primates. Once it was believed that the higher primates went through a 'platyrrhine phase' followed by a 'cercopithecoid phase' before reaching the 'hominoid phase'. The correctness of this view, however, is becoming increasingly unlikely. More probably, the New and Old World stocks evolved separately from

The relative sizes of the olfactory (left) and visual (right) centres in the brains of a lemur (1), Cercopithecus (2), and modern man (3)

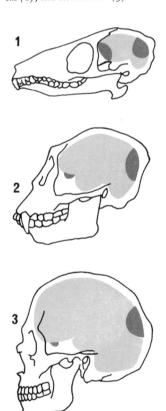

1

2

3

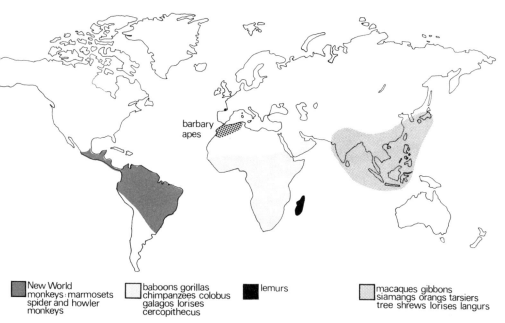

barbary apes

■ New World monkeys : marmosets spider and howler monkeys

□ baboons gorillas chimpanzees colobus galagos lorises cercopithecus

■ lemurs

▨ macaques gibbons siamangs orangs tarsiers tree shrews lorises langurs

distinct prosimian ancestors. Possibly cercopithecoids and hominoids also evolved separately–although this is perhaps unlikely. But many of the characteristics separating higher primates from Prosimii were acquired separately by platyrrhines and catarrhines, a further example of parallel evolution.

The changes in the brain of higher primates are found mainly in the cerebrum, or higher centres. This part of the brain has little to do with the basic running of the body, but rather with coping with the environment. The areas of the cerebrum associated with vision, memory, reasoning, and manipulative ability are larger than in prosimians, while the olfactory sense is relatively less important. Behaviour, both individual and social, is more complex and therefore increasingly flexible and variable. As the brain becomes bigger the skull becomes more rounded, and with the further reduction of the sense of smell the face gets still flatter. The orbits of the eyes are closed behind by bony flanges. The dentition also changes, the alterations being linked in some as yet unexplained ways to diet and feeding behaviour.

Map locating the natural habitats of the main groups of primates other than man

ORDER	**PRIMATES**	
SUBORDER	**ANTHROPOIDEA**	**PROSIMII** (lemur, indris, loris, potto, bush-baby, tarsier)
INFRAORDER	**CATARRHINI**	**PLATYRRHINI** (marmoset, tamarin, howler, capuchin, spider monkey)
SUPERFAMILY	**HOMINOIDEA**	**CERCOPITHECOIDEA** (macaque, baboon, gelada, guenon, patas monkey, langur)
FAMILY	**HOMINIDAE**	**HYLOBATIDAE** (gibbon, siamang)
		PONGIDAE (orang utan, chimpanzee, gorilla)
GENUS	*HOMO*	
SPECIES	*HOMO SAPIENS* (man)	

For our purposes the New World monkeys are not especially important animals. The first ceboids appear in the late Oligocene or early Miocene (about 25 million years ago) and at that time are already quite similar to their descendants. They are an exclusively arboreal group, and all are quadrupeds of various sorts. The more primitive ones, like the marmosets, are quadrupedal leapers and runners, and are similar to the more quadrupedal species of *Lemur*. One subfamily, the Atelinae, is of special interest, however. The spider monkey, *Ateles*, spends much of its resting time with its trunk in a vertical position. When climbing in the trees it will often pull itself up or let itself down by its arms. Sometimes it will progress by arm-swinging or brachiation, although at these times it almost always uses its powerful prehensile tail. Most of the time however it is quadrupedal, and it may even walk bipedally along branches. As in the case of *Palaeopropithecus*, *Ateles* has a number of skeletal adaptations which are thought to be associated with arm-swinging, although many may just be correlated with the trunk being more or less vertical much of the time. The arms are long, and the hands are hook-like and lack thumbs. The vertebral column is relatively short and rigid, and the chest broad and flat. The shoulder blades lie on the back of the thorax and are elongated from top to bottom rather than from side to side as in quadrupeds. Because leaping is an important part of locomotion the hindlimbs are also well developed.

What are spider monkeys to be called in locomotor terms? They have been described as 'semi-brachiators' but this kind of terminology can be more of a hindrance than a help. In terms of what they do mostly, they are quadrupeds about eighty per cent of the time, and arm-swing only about 10 per cent of the time. They are best termed arm-swinging quadrupeds. If our scheme of primate locomotor evolution from hind-limb dominated to fore-limb dominated locomotion is correct we can view *Ateles* as a kind of intermediate between quadrupeds and brachiators like the gibbons, just as *Lemur catta* represents a half-way stage between vertical

Opposite: a table summarizing the classification of primates in relation to man. Examples of genera coming under a given group heading are indicated (in brackets) by their common names

The very primitive monkey-like teeth of Parapithecus (left), dating from Oligocene times, compared with the teeth of the talapoin monkey

Ape and monkey teeth are conspicuously different. Monkey molars invariably have four cusps paired in two ridges. Ape (and human) molars generally have five cusps and no transverse ridges

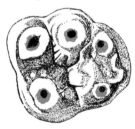

Opposite: a grivet monkey (Cercopithecus aethiops) eating fruit in an East African thorn tree

clinging and leaping, and quadrupedalism. Perhaps *Ateles* is intermediate because it fills an 'intermediate' niche between those of ordinary quadrupeds and the small branch niche of the brachiating gibbons.

Old World monkeys (Cercopithecoids) are basically a quadrupedal group, like the platyrrhines, although they have evolved ground-living forms as well. The superfamily probably appeared during the Oligocene in Africa, and may be represented in the Fayum deposits of Egypt (deposits representing a dense tropical forest ecology) by *Parapithecus*. This small form has teeth which are very primitive but which do in some ways resemble those of monkeys.

The first undoubted monkeys come from Napak in Uganda. This is an early Miocene site, with an age of about 20 million years. Unfortunately, the specimen is just a single molar although distinctive enough to be readily identifiable as monkey, and as a member of the subfamily Cercopithecinae. Monkeys do not become really abundant until the Pliocene. Why this should be so is still unknown. Hominoids of all kinds are abundant in the Miocene and lived then, like their descendants, in forested areas. Monkeys are also forest animals, so why they should not be preserved in Miocene deposits is really rather a mystery.

Although cercopithecoids and hominoids are related to each other, as comparative anatomy and biochemistry indicate, there are between them certain very distinctive contrasts. Their teeth, for instance, differ markedly; possibly the differences were originally correlated with diet. Thus it has been suggested that the earliest monkeys were herbivorous leaf-eaters, while the first hominoids were fruit-eaters. Whether this is correct or not is at present difficult to say. All cercopithecoids, like the quadrupedal prosimians or the more primitive Platyrrhines, are quadrupeds. They have long trunks with springy vertebral columns, narrow deep chests, and well developed hind-limbs for leaping. There are two basic subdivisions, usually classified as subfamilies. These are Colobinae and Cercopithecinae.

The colobines are less abundant than the cercopithecines, and are found in Africa and Asia. In general they are highly arboreal, although some species like *Presbytis entellus* spend considerable amounts of time on the ground. They have a relatively restricted diet composed mainly of leaves, augmented sometimes with other vegetable food; they possess specialized stomachs to cope with this food. They probably split from the cercopithecines early on, and it is at least a possibility that the very earliest monkeys were colobines. This is a reversal of the more generally accepted theory, but does help to make a little more sense of the facts. Originating, like all Catarrhines, in Africa, they spread to Asia probably during the first half of the Miocene, say 25 to 18 million years ago. Because the living colobines are so arboreal it would seem most plausible that at this time the land connection between Africa and Asia was forested. The colobines probably spread at about the time the lorisines did. The subfamily contains some genera–for example, *Nasalis*, which do arm-swing occasionally–but basically the colobines are arboreal quadrupeds.

The Cercopithecinae have been more successful in terms of numbers. The guenons (*Cercopithecus* species) are small- to medium-sized arboreal quadrupedal animals whose diet consists mostly of fruit and nuts. The early fossil history of cercopithecines is very sketchy but they probably first differentiated in the Miocene. The early cercopithecines probably looked like *Cercopithecus*. This subfamily is interesting here because it has produced independently at least four lineages of terrestrial quadrupeds. Because these primates are ground-dwellers in open country they occupy much the same ecological niche as early man and for this reason anthropologists have been studying their behaviour and social organization. In this way, they hope to get ideas about some of the behaviour adaptations of the first non-arboreal hominids.

One of the ground-living monkeys, *Erythrocebus*, the patas, is closely related to *Cercopithecus* and probably evolved fairly recently from this genus. Its terrestrial adaptations are distributed quite widely through the skeleton and are very similar to those found in the extinct Malagasy lemur *Hadropithecus*, a remarkable example of parallelism. The patas and the guenon are placed in one tribe (a subdivision of the Cercopithecinae) called the Cercopithecini. There are two further tribes in this subfamily. One, the Theropithecini, includes just one living species *Theropithecus gelada*, the gelada baboon. Geladas live in very arid country in Ethiopia, and again show many adaptations to ground living. Species closely related to the gelada were formerly widespread in early and middle Pleistocene deposits elsewhere in Africa. These extinct forms were generally classified as *Simopithecus*, although some workers today would prefer to treat them as a subgenus within *Theropithecus*—as *Theropithecus (Simopithecus)*. The basic population unit in geladas is a single male plus a number of females, forming a kind of 'harem'. When feeding conditions are particularly good, these units aggregate in large herds, but even then the females

A dominant male gelada baboon, his 'harem'—three females—and a baby

are still tied to 'their' male. The aggregations can be made up of a random sampling of one-male groups. Groups composed solely of males are also found from time to time. These single male groups probably represent one way of responding to a particularly inhospitable environment. Interestingly enough, the patas also lives in single male social groups, although patas 'leading males' are far less tolerant of each other than gelada males.

The third tribe, the Cercocebini, is the one of most interest. For our purposes, the most important animals are those of the baboon-macaque group because they have been studied in most detail. *Papio* is closely related to *Macaca*, although species of *Papio* are more closely related to each other than they are to *Macaca* species. Species in these two genera, plus the mangabeys (*Cercocebus*), are anatomically and genetically very similar. They all have 42 chromosomes, and their basic

Opposite: an Ethiopian gelada baboon expressing aggression and fear by flipping back its upper lip, exposing its teeth and entirely covering its nose. Above: a patas monkey (Erythrocebus), sitting in the road near the Murchison Falls, Uganda

Overleaf: Rhesus monkeys leaping across the 12-foot gap between two rocks in their enclosure at London Zoo ►

53

behavioural repertoire in terms of postures, facial expressions, reproductive behaviour, and so forth is essentially similar. Baboons, macaques and mangabeys are split into a number of very closely related species. Either these species have but recently split or the rate of evolution has not been particularly rapid, because species within and between these genera are fully interfertile with each other. *Papio*, in particular, is a constellation of very similar species which are either speciating now or have just speciated.

Baboons

Baboon species are distributed throughout most of sub-Saharan Africa in savannah regions, and the woodland and forested areas adjacent to this. One species, *Papio hamadryas*, is found in arid country in Ethiopia; the other closely related species cover the rest of the range. In places these species merge, in others they behave like 'good' species. All this points to the very close genetical relationship of all baboon species.

The savannah baboons have been until recently the most closely studied of all the African monkeys. Pioneering work by Professors Washburn and DeVore in East Africa and the late Professor Hall in South Africa has clarified many features of baboon life in open country. Savannah baboons live in more or less closed social groups, and only rarely switch from one troop to another. The social group is of the utmost

Baboons on the move. The two large dominant males have taken up positions near the centre of the troop, close to the juveniles and females with babies. Subordinate males travel at the head and rear of the troop and give warning of danger

importance to survival. Each troop has a 'home range' through which it moves. Home ranges of adjacent troops overlap, although each has a central 'core area' which does not. There is marked contrast in body size and behaviour between males and females, and this is reflected in their roles. The males are about twice the size of the females, and have enormous canines. The rest of the teeth are also large (necessary for feeding a big body), and so the face is long and projecting ('prognathous'). The females have small canines, scarcely projecting beyond the level of the other teeth. These differences are a good example of structural differences between the sexes of the same species ('sexual dimorphism'). They are contrasts which appear gradually and in their final form only after sexual maturity. The morphological differences reflect behavioural differences, males being much more aggressive animals responsible for troop defence. The open country habitat, it is argued, poses a large number of problems in the way of predators, and so males need to be relatively aggressive and the troop must be rather tightly organized. Social life within the troop is quite tense, and this tension is expressed as aggressive behaviour which could be potentially disruptive to the troop unless channelled and dealt with.

Dominance hierarchies are clear-cut among these animals, and tend to be linear. That is, animal A is dominant to animal B in almost all situations, animal B to C, and so forth. These relationships can be more subtle than this, with shifting alliances between animals. Thus B and C might together displace A in a given situation. The aggressive, or 'agonistic', interactions between adult males very rarely involves physical fighting—indeed the hierarchy probably reduces fighting. Dominance relationships among males are worked out during early life by play fighting, at a stage when the animals can do each other little actual harm. Adult males can, in their role as troop peace-keepers, break up dangerous fights. Dominance interactions in adult life are based mainly on facial and vocal displays and on postures, and rely upon each animal 'knowing its

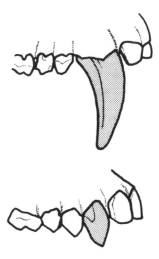

The relatively enormous canine teeth of a male baboon compared with those of a female

A baboon troop in the trees. Although habitually terrestrial, baboons will climb trees with alacrity if threatened, or in order to sleep in safety at night

place' (although its place obviously changes with time). The dominant males 'police' the troop, act as sentinels, break up fights, look after females with young infants, and generally keep things going smoothly. One should really regard dominance relations of this sort not as something utterly basic but as a result of the very necessary aggressiveness of male savannah baboons.

The troop sleeps in trees during the night or, rarely, on cliffs in areas where trees are not readily available. Trees are sought too in times of danger, so there is still a premium on climbing abilities. Baboons sleep sitting with trunks erect. They have hardened pads on their buttocks, as an adaptation to this. A good deal of waking time is spent sitting erect too–in grooming, for example. Leaving the trees, the troop moves out early in the day in search of food and water. It travels in fairly regular order, with females and infants surrounded by dominant males. If the troop is disturbed, it will retreat in order, the males bringing up the rear. Food is mostly vegetable, and almost any vegetable food will do. Sometimes males will kill and eat other animals, generally young antelope. This predatory behaviour is most common in the wet season when the young of the prey have just been born.

Baboons are sexually promiscuous animals. Females go through an oestrus cycle, a period of sexual receptivity at the time of ovulation, when the female actively solicits males. Females will copulate with progessively more dominant males as they come into oestrus. At the peak of oestrus they will go to the periphery of the troop with a dominant male forming there a 'consort pair'. Consort pairs rarely stay together more than a few days, during which time sexual and grooming behaviours are frequent. Impregnation of females tends therefore to be by those males which are most dominant at that particular time. Mothers with infants are highly prized and protected, and act as centres of attraction to other females (and even males) who want to groom them. Threatened males may even use infants as protection against more dominant baboons! The infant stays close to its mother until it is weaned during its second year. Eventually mother–infant ties become very loose and the young baboon tends to spend more and more time playing in its peer group.

Grooming is important on all sorts of occasions and the desire to groom and be groomed is as much built into the animal as the drive that makes a sick animal keep up with the troop for as long as possible. (This desire of one primate for contact with others has been used in psychological experiments. Instead of a food reward for successfully doing the required tasks, the sight of another monkey is provided.) Grooming is done with the hands, fingers and thumbs being used actively to pick through the fur. In prosimians grooming is done with the teeth, while in New World monkeys the fingers are dragged more or less passively through the fur. The baboons, being terrestrial animals, have evolved extremely dexterous hands. The index finger can be moved independently as well as the thumb, and this is due to the selective pressures for efficient food manipulation, as well as grooming. From small beginnings, the grasping prosimian hand was pre-adapted to become ever more dexterous and to function in ever more complicated ways.

Laboratory experiments show that young monkeys reared in isolation from their mothers are highly disturbed psychologically. In adulthood, for example, they may not know how to copulate. When adult, the females make bad mothers, ignoring their infants or even causing them physical harm. These experiments underline what is apparent from studies in the wild – the tremendous importance to individual primates of socializing. Learning clearly plays a very important part in the life of the individual and the group. Just how great a part was perhaps not fully realized until the primate field studies of the last fifteen years began to throw light on the amazing complexity of primate social life. Learning in baboons, as in all primates, is not generalized. A species learns some things more easily than others. Individuals acquire best those skills that are useful in their particular adaptive situation, and the practice and acquisition of these skills is pleasurable to them. Male patas, for example, learn to flee from the bigger cats to distract them while the patas females and young 'freeze'. Male savannah baboons on the other hand will collectively face up to cheetahs or leopards. The troop is protected in each case, but male behaviour contrasts markedly; for each species, the behaviour is appropriate and adaptive.

Recently, Dr Thelma Rowell has been studying forest-dwelling baboons in Uganda, baboons of the same species as some of those savannah-dwellers we have just discussed. Her results are very illuminating. It seems that under savannah conditions there are a great many opportunities for inter-individual interactions. Without a fairly strict dominance hierarchy there would be constant fighting, so dominance ranking is a process of stabilizing these interrelationships

Common to all primates is the need for social links with others of the same species to be constantly reinforced, preferably by actual bodily contact. To answer to this need is one of the chief functions of grooming activity (illustrated opposite). Monkeys reared under socially deprived conditions may behave abnormally. Below, a mother, so reared, rejects her infant

and thus of avoiding fighting as much as possible. Also, congregation around desired food sources tends to produce fighting and hence the appearance to the observer of a more rigid hierarchy than in fact exists. (So if observers use food to attract animals the better to watch them, some of the observations may be biased.) The earlier baboon work before Dr Rowell's suggested that all baboons were at all times rigidly hierarchical. Her later studies of forest baboons show that behaviour is by no means fixed and static within a species. In forest environments food is more readily available than in the savannah, without so much competition. Predators are not so common, and social life is far from tense. Agonistic behaviour is considerably less frequent and the rigid dominance hierarchy of males, once thought to be so typical, is not present in the forest. The males behave as a sort of club, and act as 'policemen'. If the troop is disturbed, it is often a case of 'mothers and children last'! The troops are not tightly closed units either and there is frequent interchange of individuals between groups. So, many of the generalizations derived from the savannah studies do not apply to the species as a whole, and this points up the great effects of environment on behaviour. Clearly the environment in which learning occurs influences exactly what is learned. Savannah and woodland primates tend to live in larger and more structured social groups than do arboreal primates. Their diet tends to become more omnivorous, and there are many other changes in behaviour. The animals are more dexterous, their facial and vocal communications tend to be more complex, and their home-ranges are larger.

Macaques

Macaques have also been studied in detail. Much of the work has been on Japanese macaques, studied over a period of fifteen years or so. Much of their social behaviour has been distorted because animals are fed in a particular place to make observation easier, and consequently fighting is abnormally frequent in these crowded situations. However, some of the more detailed aspects of inter-individual behaviour have been revealed in these and other studies. One particularly interesting point is that there are kinship ties of sorts between females and their offspring–these ties being stronger for female young. (Since these animals are promiscuous, there can be no paternal ties in non-human primates.) Female offspring tend to stay close to their mothers, and as adults to consort with them. The mother's dominance status affects the ultimate status of her daughter. Among males, grooming pairs often turn out to be 'brothers' (sons of the same mother). Macaque troops may also develop traditions. One Japanese troop developed the habit of washing sweet-potatoes in streams and in the sea. The males of some troops play frequently with infants; the males of other troops may ignore babies entirely. All in all, behavioural contrasts between troops may be quite marked and can be considered as rudimentary cultural, or proto-cultural, differences.

In summary, we can see the cercopithecoids as a highly successful group of primates, originating in Africa at least 30 or 40 million years ago, and becoming since then steadily more diversified. Initially an herbivorous, arboreal stock, they later developed more omnivorous, terrestrial (as opposed to arboreal) lineages. These lineages evolved social structures which are highly complex. The ground-living cercopithecoids can perhaps tell us something about higher primate social structure under open country conditions, but it would be dangerous to assume that the earliest savannah-dwelling hominids would have necessarily behaved like baboons simply because they occupied similar niches. Hominids are more closely related to the apes, and it is to them that we turn now.

Macaque monkeys at the Japan Monkey Centre at Inuyama have acquired a habit of carefully washing sweet potatoes in sea water before eating them

Gibbons

The superfamily of Hominoidea contains the lesser apes (gibbons and siamangs), the great apes, and man, together with their fossil ancestors. It is variously divided (partly according to taste) because the gibbons now appear to be the termination of a very ancient lineage, I prefer to separate them as a family. All three families share a basic dental structure, in which they contrast with monkeys. Possibly the first hominoids separated from the first monkeys by becoming fruit-eaters (the monkeys being leaf-eaters). First, however, we shall consider the living species before adding the fossils to the final picture.

The Hylobatidae (gibbons and siamangs) are divided into two similar genera, *Hylobates* and *Symphalangus*. *Hylobates* is better known and will be taken as our example. In their social behaviour, the gibbons are somewhat aberrant among hominoids, living in small family groups consisting of male and female plus offspring. The 'pair-bond' (the sexual tie between adult

male and adult female) seems to last for life. This grouping resembles in superficial organization the basic human family, but the resemblance is purely fortuitous and has no importance. Ancestral gibbons almost certainly did not have this peculiar social structure. Males and females are of about the same size, each weighing about 15 pounds (baboon male, 70 pounds; baboon female, 35 pounds), and both have large, projecting canines, an unusual feature among primates, as mostly males only have the large canines. Gibbons are territorial, each social group defending a tiny quarter-square-mile territory that has definite boundaries and into which no other group is allowed. Gibbons are one of the few truly territorial primates, most of the others living within a rather less precise home-range. The male gibbon defends his territorial boundaries against adjacent males by actual physical fighting. Much of the gibbon display behaviour–breaking off and throwing branches, for example–is similar to that of other hominoids, and contrasts with monkey behaviour. Gibbons are the least intelligent of hominoids, but are nevertheless very clever animals, performing well in psychological tests. They are the brachiators *par excellence*, progressing rapidly beneath branches using their arms alone extended above their head, and they cross wide gaps in this way too. Like other hominoids they lack tails. 'Brachiator', however, describes what the gibbon does far less well than the term 'quadruped' describes what a baboon does, because the gibbons spend time climbing quadrupedally and running along branches bipedally. Brachiation alone is in fact an inefficient method of moving for long distances; perhaps there is a correlation here between small territory and brachiation. Brachiation is useful as a means of getting out into the periphery of the tree by grasping supports instead of standing on them, in order to feed in the outer branches. As I have said, spider monkeys do this part of the time and hence are partly like gibbons.

The skeletal adaptations to the locomotor or feeding behaviour are widespread and similar to those listed for spider monkeys. The trunk is short, the chest wide and

Most expert of all brachiators, the gibbon is able to swing itself through a tree's outermost branches with complete assurance. Opposite and left: a gibbon brachiating and at rest

65

shallow. Flexion and extension of the back in locomotion are unimportant and so the back can be rigid with muscles reduced. The arms are long and mobile with hands and fingers long and curved. Unlike the spider monkey's, the gibbon's thumb is well developed because selection pressures for manipulation, feeding and grooming are sufficiently strong. The legs, although short relative to the arms, are still quite long compared to trunk length. When gibbons move on top of supports or on the ground (mostly in zoos) they tend to be bipedal. This is possibly because the trunk is held erect during brachiation and climbing and this preadapts the animal for bipedal walking with the body kept erect. The same applies for the spider monkey.

For a long time it has been assumed that the similarities between gibbons and man (or other hominoids) imply a close evolutionary relationship, all of them being evolved from a common ancestor looking like a gibbon and possessing a constellation of 'hominoid' adaptations. The similarities are generally in chest and trunk, all hominoids including man having a short lumbar region of the backbone, and a broad, shallow chest with the shoulder blades displaced on to the back. However, many of the similarities might be parallelisms, and if the fossil record of gibbons is examined, it can be seen that this may well be the case.

The earliest hylobatids, like all Catarrhines, occur in Africa and are found in the Fayum Oligocene deposits in Egypt. One jaw of the genus *Aeolopithecus* may be that of a gibbon ancestor; nothing is known of the rest of its skeleton. Later, gibbon-like animals are found in the Miocene of East Africa, in Uganda as early as about 22 million years ago, and as late as 14 million years ago in Kenya. The fossils have been classified in various species of the genus *Limnopithecus*. *Limnopithecus* is a very interesting animal, having teeth and skull very reminiscent of the gibbons, while the skeleton is quite different. Although the skeleton foreshadows the condition of later hylobatids, it is much more primitive. Arms and legs are of nearly equal length and the animal was clearly an arboreal quadruped, perhaps

As the early, small anthropoid ape Limnopithecus might have appeared: a gibbon-like creature, but without the extremely long arms of the modern gibbon

rather like *Ateles*, possibly doing some arm-swinging. Probably *Limnopithecus* was less restricted in its group range than *Hylobates*, and perhaps lived in larger troops.

At some time during the Miocene, hylobatids invaded Europe and Asia. They are known from Europe as *Pliopithecus*, although this genus is closely related to *Limnopithecus* and is probably descended from it. The spread occurred no doubt at the time of the lorisid and colobine invasion when the linking area was forested. As the Eurasian landmass became less forested during the Pliocene and Pleistocene, hylobatids became confined to Southeast Asia where they live today. Hylobatids had become extinct in Africa by the Pliocene, possibly because of competition from cercopithecines. This could account too for their shrinking distribution in the Eurasian Pliocene. Brachiating gibbons seem therefore to have evolved from quadrupedal forerunners after these ancestors diverged from other hominoids. The similarities between gibbons and at least the other apes must include many parallelisms. Let us turn to these apes individually.

Orang utans and gorillas

The orang utan, *Pongo Pygmaeus*, is now largely confined to Borneo, although earlier in the Pleistocene the same species lived in Indochina and China. Before that its ancestors were even more widespread. Orangs are creatures of thick tropical rain forest, and as this type of habitat has shrunk, so too has the orang range. Moreover, they have been hunted vigorously by man, and the present-day population is very sparse. They are difficult to observe, and their behaviour is now quite aberrant. Originally they were perhaps behaviourally rather like chimpanzees, for Dr Vernon Reynolds has noted that the two species are remarkably similar in their behavioural development and in the way they solve problems. Both show a high degree of manual dexterity. Orangs are fruit-eaters and spend their time almost wholly in the trees. They are deliberate climbers and often hang by their arms; they can brachiate but are generally quadrumanous. They have very long

An orang utan, hanging by an arm from a forest tree in Borneo, uses both hands and feet to steady his favourite food, a durian fruit, said to taste like almond-flavoured custard with sherry added

A gorilla yawns (opposite) and adopts a characteristic knuckle-walking posture (below)

arms with long, curved hands. Their legs are short but mobile too, and their feet are long and curved, just like the hands. Each night they build and sleep in a new nest.

The African *Gorilla gorilla* is solely a forest-dweller. It is the largest of the primates and spends a great deal of its adult life on the forest floor. Gorillas have been described as 'modified brachiators', but in fact rarely if ever brachiate, then only as infants. The discrepancy arises because primatologists have sometimes classified gorillas and gibbons in the same locomotor group because of their skeletal similarities. Yet gibbons are unusual primates and should not be used as a yardstick; and there is also clearly the possibility that some of the so-called 'brachiating features' of gorillas have little or nothing to do with brachiating at all, but have developed for other reasons.

Strictly speaking, gorillas are 'knuckle-walking quadrupeds', walking on the backs of the middle parts of the third and fourth fingers of each hand. The fingers, hand, wrist, arm and arm joints are all adapted to this type of locomotion which is used in the trees as well as on the ground. The foot shows some parallel trends in the human direction to ground-walking. Unlike the other hominoids, gorillas are herbivores rather than fruit-eaters; this is correlated with their terrestrial way of life. They live in small groups and are rather phlegmatic and tolerant animals; their behaviour has been delightfully described by Schaller. As with orangs and chimps, gorillas build nests, though mostly on the ground. This nest building behaviour is partly innate, partly learned, as has been shown by comparison of zoo- with field-studied animals.

The gorilla can teach two important lessons. First, that appearances can be deceptive. The Victorians believed that because gorillas were large, fearsome-looking animals, they must be instinctive, savage beasts, the perfect antithesis of rational man. Nothing, of course, could be further from the truth and it is actual field studies on gorillas (as well as other monkeys and apes) which have helped to correct this false impression. Second, the gorilla shows how confusing it can be to classify locomotor behaviour on morphology rather than on actual observed behaviour. Dr Alan Walker has suggested the following tentative explanation for some features of the gorilla skeleton. The 'brachiating' adaptations of gorillas seem to be, in the main, adaptations for clambering and climbing with much of the weight being borne by the arms in pulling the body up and letting it down. Lengthening of the arms is found in other ground-living forms, and this may be a partial explanation of the gorilla's long arms. Because of these climbing adaptations the gorilla's shoulder joint is very mobile and the young therefore are able occasionally to brachiate. They are, in this sense, preadapted for it. This is an unorthodox view, implying that gorillas never went through a gibbon-like brachiating stage. Possibly their ancestors were mobile-limbed quadrupeds, though it is likely that arm-swinging formed a larger part of proto-gorilla behaviour.

Chimpanzees

The chimpanzee, *Pan troglodytes*, is perhaps the best known of all primates and a great favourite in zoos. These are inhabitants of the tropical African forest, and are found also in open woodland on the forest fringes. In thick forest they may spend up to 80 per cent of their time feeding in the trees, mainly on fruits. There they may hang from their arms, occasionally moving by arm-swinging, climb quadrupedally, and knuckle-walk or move bipedally along branches. They also come to the ground a great deal, particularly in open woodland. They are best regarded as both arboreal and terrestrial animals; when startled in the trees they will often

A group of mountain gorillas resting in a moss-covered tree in the rain forests of central Africa

descend to the ground, escaping along pathways there. On the ground they are knuckle-walking quadrupeds although they are bipedal too on occasion. As in the gorilla, adaptations to knuckle-walking are widespread in the fore-limb and this has led some workers to infer that the common ancestors of chimps and gorillas were knuckle-walkers too. Yet we have already seen how widespread parallelism is among primates. Terrestrial quadrupedalism with similar adaptations has evolved four times among cercopithecoids and twice among Madagascar lemurs. To derive knuckle-walking independently in two lines need therefore pose no great theoretical problem.

Chimpanzee social life is now quite well understood, owing mainly to the fascinating research of Jane van Lawick-Goodall in Tanzania since 1960. Further important work has been done by the Reynoldses, by Kortlandt, and by Japanese workers. Chimps apparently live in troops of between 20 and 50 animals. Within these troops they form small groups of varying composition; the most basic group consists of females or females plus offspring. Adult females spending much time together often turn out to be mother and daughter, or sisters. Mother and offspring live together consistently, at least for the first four or five years of life, longer

A mother chimpanzee protectively nurses her infant. The tie between a baby chimp and its mother is more enduring than in any other primate except man

The daily chimpanzees' tea-party at London Zoo serves not only to divert visitors, but also to engage the chimpanzees' own considerable intelligence and so prevent boredom

A rudimentary sense of composition is evident in this painting by a chimpanzee at London Zoo. Perhaps most remarkable, however, is the enthusiasm and perseverence that chimpanzee painters often evince

than in any other primate except man. During this time the young learn from their mother and from other chimps all the complicated acquired behaviours of chimpanzee adult life. Life for the young chimpanzee is relaxed and tolerant, and an infant will spend much of its time playing with other infants, with its mother and with its brothers and sisters. After this five year initial period, contacts with the mother are still maintained, particularly by daughters. Even sons return from time to time from their wanderings to greet their mothers affectionately. This is important because it means that these simple kinship ties – mother/daughter, mother/son, sister/brother (still no father!) – are recognized, even though the animals are not constantly near to one another. Male chimpanzees sometimes move with females, although often they will travel in all-male groups from one food source area to another, and are generally the first to locate choice new localities for fruits. When a new feeding area is found, other chimps are attracted by drumming and shouting.

In open woodland, troops of 40 or so animals may have home ranges of up to 80 square miles or more, much larger than in any other non-human primate.

The Japanese work in Tanzania has suggested the possibility that the maturing males of one troop may leave that troop and join another, being replaced in their turn by males from other groups. If this should turn out to be the case, we should have more insight into the possible origins of incest taboos.

Chimps are obviously highly intelligent animals and psychological tests in laboratories on these apes, and indeed on all the pongids, only confirm just how intelligent they are. Their behaviour is, in general, less stereotyped than that of cercopithecoids. Problem solving is by hypothesis-testing, rather than by trial and error. All in all, we are dealing with animals in which there are glimpses of ourselves as yet unevolved, so to speak.

The females have a typical oestrus cycle and cyclical sexual receptivity. Dominance interactions are not particularly marked and in no way affect an individual's access to females. The same applies to gorillas and probably to orangs too. It is probable that mating between mother and son does not occur; the occurrence of sexual relations between brothers and sisters is also doubtful. Perhaps familiarity breeds contempt for chimps as well as humans!

In the forest chimps are predominantly fruit-eaters (upon occasion they are cannibalistic!), but in open woodland they may add more protein to their diet. Males sometimes kill colobus monkeys or bush-pig; often males will gang up in a group to achieve their ends. Meat is a very choice item in chimpanzee diet and is eaten slowly and deliberately with a mouthful of leaves between each bite. It is sometimes shared out with other chimps who will beg for pieces. This food-sharing is very unusual among non-human primates; mostly it is every primate for himself. When the season is right chimps in woodland also eat termites, and they do this by 'fishing' for them. When beginning a bout of termiting, an animal will carefully select stems or pieces of grass, trim them to the appropriate length, collect enough of them, and set out on the hunt for insects. It may pass over several termite hills if they are

A chimpanzee quickly learns how to open a locked and bolted safe

not ready and go on until it finds a mound ripe for fishing. Using a finger, a hole is scraped and the prepared twig inserted. Withdrawn covered with termites, it is passed carefully over the lower lip until every delicious morsel is removed, and the operation repeated. Clearly, in doing so, chimps are taking natural objects, modifying them to a standard pattern and using them for an objective which involves planning and forethought. They are, in fact, making tools. This has surprised many people, for previously man was considered to be the only tool-maker. In the chimpanzee, however, the intellectual abilities necessary for purposive tool-making are already developed at an infrahuman level. Other examples of chimp tool-use in natural surroundings have also been seen. For instance, chewed leaves are used as sponges to soak up water from holes in trees. They are also used to wipe dung or mud from the body. Stones and branches are used too in agonistic displays or when an animal is excited. They may be thrown under- or over-arm, often with considerable force and accuracy. Similar behaviour has been observed in other apes. Stones are used to open nuts too.

There are some further peculiarities of ape behaviour which are quite fascinating. Jane van Lawick-Goodall once observed a chimpanzee sitting, apparently transfixed, watching a beautiful African sunset. Can chimps have aesthetic tastes? Examples of ape art in zoos would suggest that this is certainly the case. In London Zoo chimps have learned how to paint, always with a detectable individualistic style. They can match the compositional abilities of a three-year-old human child, before the first diagramatic representation of the face. Painting is to a high degree 'autotelic', that is to say, self-rewarding. Ape painters hate being interrupted, even for food! Jane van Lawick-Goodall has also seen what she calls a 'rain-dance', an energetic and rhythmic series of movements performed by males, watched by excited females, when there is a tropical rainstorm.

The living non-human hominoids are characterized by certain behavioural features which are not found in

An orang utan 'artist' at the easel

other primates. We can see in these the analogues of many human characteristics previously considered specifically human.

Comparative anatomy and biochemistry indicate that the chimp and gorilla are in many respects more similar to each other than they are to the orang. It is becoming increasingly probable that the orang is more distantly related (in terms of recency of common ancestry) to either African ape than is man. It certainly is obvious that the apes are morphologically and behaviourally all rather similar, while man is distinctly different, and hence it is most sensible to classify all three great apes in one family, separate from Hominidae.

Sites of dryopithecine (fossil-ape) finds in the Old World

Professor Elwyn Simons and the skull of Aegyptopithecus zeuxis, which he discovered in the Fayum deposits, about 60 miles southwest of Cairo

Fossil apes

What of the fossil record? A great amount of energy has been expended on trying to unravel ape evolution, often with precious little result. The first fossil ape, *Dryopithecus fontani*, was recovered from middle Miocene French deposits in 1856 and was known to, and mentioned by, Darwin. This genus became the type of the subfamily Dryopithecinae. Over the years large numbers of new dryopithecines have been found from various areas of the Old World. Unfortunately, almost every new specimen was given a new name (rather like a first name and surname!) without proper regard either for the rules of naming or for zoological common sense.

Until the 1960s, more than 50 species and 20 genera had been described. This gave the impression that a huge multiplicity of apes had swarmed all over the Old World during the later Tertiary. However, careful examination of these specimens by Professor Elwyn Simons of Yale University and myself showed (for us, at any rate!) a rather different picture. (An account of our work is available in some detail elsewhere.)

The earliest known dryopithecine is *Aegyptopithecus zeuxis*, found by Elwyn Simons in the Fayum Oligocene deposits of the Egyptian desert. It is probably 28 or 30 million years old. Its dentition is typically pongid and some specimens (? males) have large projecting canines. The teeth are primitive in a number of features. The skull is most interesting, being not ape-ish but rather more like a monkey's or even a prosimian's. Superficially it looks like some of the Malagasy sub-fossil lemur skulls. (Why is perhaps not hard to see.) The snout is rather long and there is a hint of a crest on the skull for attaching the chewing muscles, a sign that the brain is relatively small; when the braincase is small and chewing muscles are large, a crest is built along the top of the skull to provide extra areas of muscle attachment (this occurs in similar circumstances in numerous mammals, including dogs). Not much of the skeleton has been found, but what there is tells us much. *Aegyptopithecus* had a tail, and the hands and feet of a typical

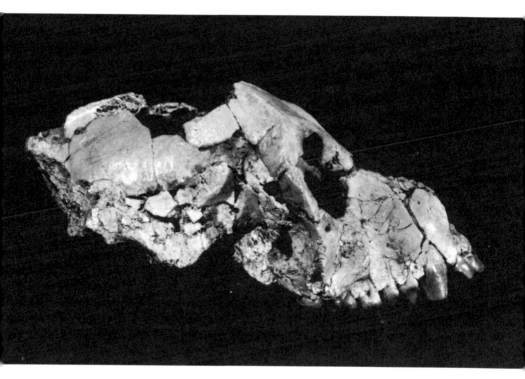

arboreal quadruped (like one of the more arboreal *Cercopithecus* species).

The next dryopithecines are also African and are found in East Africa in Kenya and Uganda. Several hundred specimens have been recovered, mainly due to the tremendous efforts of the indefatigable Dr Louis Leakey. First to be described were species of a genus originally termed *Proconsul*. At one time some workers, including Dr Leakey, regarded these apes as being close to human ancestry, but this now seems improbable. Many of the supposed specializations of *Proconsul*, which made it different from other dryopithecines, are now known to be merely primitive features, and *Proconsul* is best treated simply as an early dryopithecine. Professor Simons and I believe that *Proconsul* species should be transferred to *Dryopithecus*, since all species of both groups differ no more than do species of *Hylobates* for instance, or *Macaca*. Even if the name

The skull of Aegyptopithecus zeuxis, the most primitive dryopithecine fossil yet discovered. Its owner lived some 28 million years ago

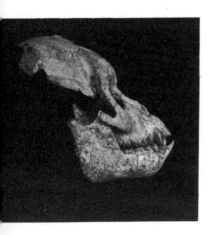

The crushed skull of Dryopithecus (Proconsul) africanus, discovered on Rusinga Island in Lake Victoria Nyanza. Originally it was thought to belong to an ancestor of man

Opposite: Dryopithecus (Proconsul) as he might have appeared in the environs of East Africa some 15–25 million years ago

Proconsul is retained, it should be remembered that it is a genus very closely related to Dryopithecus. However, I shall treat it as a subgenus of Dryopithecus–D. (Proconsul).

As the story appears now, at least four D. (Proconsul) species are known from earlier Miocene deposits ranging in age from around 20 to perhaps 17 million years ago. Of these species one, D. africanus, is small and is possibly ancestral to the chimpanzee. The skull and dentition are primitive; the teeth, particularly the incisors, are small. In chimps the incisor teeth are relatively huge, a feature perhaps related to their fruit-eating diet. Because teeth and chewing muscles are small in the extinct species and because the brain is expanded beyond the Aegyptopithecus level, the brain-case is relatively rounded. This is a function of brain size, and tooth size, not evidence of any special relationship to man. This is a good example of how important it is to consider function when assessing evolutionary relationships.

The skeleton of this dryopithecine is the best understood of all fossil pongids, arm bones and part of the foot being known. D. africanus seems to have been, like Aegyptopithecus zeuxis, an arboreal quadruped. Indeed the matchable bones of the two species are almost identical, except that D. africanus is bigger. There are, however, some features of the arm which suggest the incipient development of some of the climbing and swinging adaptations found in chimps–although D. africanus was probably shorter-armed and more like a monkey. Moreover, some features of the hand and lower arm suggest perhaps a few ground-living adaptations. Possibly, therefore, D. africanus was an arboreal quadrupedal form doing some arm-swinging, but also at times coming to the ground like some of the more terrestrial Cercopithecus species (for example, the vervets). It was not a knuckle-walker.

D. (Proconsul) nyanzae was a larger species which appears to have become extinct without issue. It is closely related to a third and still larger species, D. major, and possibly resembles the common ancestor of

nyanzae and *major*. *D. major* is a very interesting form. It is known from a fair variety of bones and teeth. The face and dentition are very reminiscent of the gorilla, although the extinct form is rather smaller. Living gorillas are strongly sexually dimorphic; males are much larger than females and have long, projecting canines not present in the females. *D. major* appears to have been similarly dimorphic both in general size and in canine size. The male *D. major* was bigger than a large male chimp, the females about female chimp size. The gorilla has cheek teeth with high, pointed cusps, presumably as an adaptation to its herbivorous diet. *D. major* had lower-crowned teeth although in some features they foreshadow the gorilla condition. Similarly there are a number of facial features which, although primitive, are nevertheless remarkably reminiscent of a gorilla. In fact, *D. major* makes a very good ancestor for the living ape.

The skeleton of *D. major* is not particularly well known, but this form was quite likely some kind of quadruped. Possibly it would have been rather less arboreal than *D. africanus*, perhaps approaching the chimpanzee in some ways. Whether or not it was a knuckle-walker is unknown at present, but it is possible. *D. major* is known so far from sites which were, during the Miocene, on the thickly forested slopes of active volcanoes, a habitat quite like that of some present-day mountain gorillas. It is possible that it was already specializing towards a herbivorous diet and increasing in body size while becoming gradually more terrestrial. *D. africanus* on the other hand seems to come from a rather wider variety of ecological settings and was perhaps, like the chimpanzee, more widespread, but still confined to west and central Africa.

Chimps and gorillas have always been referred to as very close relatives; some workers would have them splitting as late as the Pleistocene. The fossil evidence, as I have shown, is rather against this; once again it looks as though two species of living hominoids have evolved their special hominoid features separately and in parallel—just like the gibbons. Unless that is so, *D.*

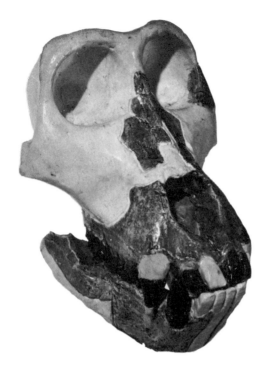

A restored fragment of the gorilla-like skull of Dryopithecus major

africanus and *D. major* are lineages paralleling chimpanzee and gorilla, but much earlier in time; this seems unlikely.

We therefore have at least two living apes accounted for as far as their fossil history is concerned. What about the third, the orang utan? There are no higher primates at all recorded in Europe or Asia before the middle Miocene—tentatively dated at about 15 or 16 million years ago. About this time a land link between Africa and Eurasia (regarded as one block since Europe is merely an Asian peninsula) permitted faunal exchange between the continents and at that time many primate lineages invaded Eurasia. As I have already noted, these included arboreal forms like the lorisids, the colobines, and the hylobatids. The orang utan is a highly arboreal animal, and presumably its ancestors were too, so the late Miocene could well have been about the latest chance for proto-orangs to leave Africa, where they must have originated. After the middle Miocene forests began to shrink, and the terrain became inhospitable in the area linking Africa and Asia.

I have already mentioned the presence in Europe during the Miocene of an ape species, *D. fontani*. This species, or one like it, continued in Europe into the early Pliocene, presumably until the habitat became completely unsuitable for apes. There were forms closely related to *D. fontani* in Asia too. Numerous dryopithecines have been recovered from deposits in the foothills of the Himalayas in northwestern India and western Pakistan. Similar forms are known too from China. They range in age from middle Miocene to early Pliocene, just as in Europe. Their absolute age we can only guess at now, but if we say 16 million to 8 million years, we shall not be far wrong. No more than three species are known from India. One is a medium-sized ape, and is extremely similar to a fragment of a jaw from a Kenyan site at Fort Ternan dated as about 14 million years old. Other evidence from the two areas also points to faunal links between the areas at this time.

Another Indian species, *D. sivalensis*, is of interest to us for it contains numerous specimens of medium- to large-sized apes, showing about the same amount of sexual dimorphism – particularly in canine size – as orangs do. There are only a few features in which *D. sivalensis* resembles the orang, but there are as yet no other good candidates for orang ancestry. Let us regard *D. sivalensis* as a possible ancestor, although not as good a one as we should like. *D. fontani* and *D. sivalensis*, the European and Asian species, are very closely related to each other, at least as close as any two baboon species. A few skeletal bones of the European form are known; they resemble some of the *D. (Proconsul)* bones and come from arboreal quadrupeds.

Very recently Dr Leakey has suggested that a fourth species from the early Miocene of Kenya is a hominid, a human ancestor. Dentally, however, this animal shows only features typical of apes, and none that are specific indicators of hominid relationships. The limb bones too are those of apes. So we are certainly dealing with an ape-like creature. It might be ancestral to later hominids (this would mean of course that at this time early hominids did not have any of the detectable specializations of later ones) but no evidence has been produced to prove this. Even if it is ancestral to hominids, it is still just like an ape and is better classified as such.

What about the possible links between this particular ape and the later Eurasian dryopithecines? *D. fontani* and *D. sivalensis* are the first Eurasian forms; they must have had ancestors in earlier African deposits. Examining some specimens of Dr Leakey's supposed hominid, it is possible to find a number of resemblances to the Eurasian forms, and these similarities could indicate an evolutionary relationship. (This is not a novel idea. When first described by Professor Le Gros Clark and Dr Leakey, the African species was tentatively considered as an ancestor of the Asian dryopithecines.) To recap, therefore, most known dryopithecines are arboreal quadrupeds, although some of them show hints of ground-living adaptations. Since their discovery, these apes have been regarded as a very complex group, splitting and radiating in all directions. It has also generally been considered probable that early human ancestors were dryopithecines. Today it is possible to tell a more accurate story. The dryopithecines were *not* startlingly diversified, and they did include the early ancestors of the three living great apes, although not apparently those of man. They originated in Africa during the Oligocene and some migrated elsewhere later in their evolution. At the time of their divergence, the species leading to the three living pongids seem to have been quadrupeds and did not resemble their descendants. This suggests that many of the similarities among living apes are probably parallelisms—a most important point.

Quadrupedalism is part of the general primate locomotion trend from vertical clinging and leaping to more fore-limb dominated methods of climbing, feeding and moving. From our study of primates it is probable that human ancestors early on would have

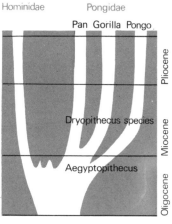

A tentative scheme of Pongid evolution during the past 30 million years

passed through a vertical clinging and leaping stage. Although we do not know for certain, it seems highly probable that they became arboreal quadrupeds. At the time of their split from the other hominoids–which was probably ancient–the hominids would have been quadrupeds of some sort. We can infer some general things about their social behaviour from primate studies. They would have been living in quite complex social groups composed of males, females and offspring. Probably the groups would have been open–exchanging individuals, particularly males–rather than closed, and dominance relationships would not have been especially marked.

Apes and men share many peculiar behavioural features which other primates lack. Possibly these are primitive (although they could be parallelisms just like some morphological features), and possibly they were shared by the earliest hominids. Some of these can be listed. Early hominids would not have had fixed territories but would have been more nomadic, moving through a home-range as different food sources became available. The basic social unit would be centred on the mother. There would be some freedom of choice in sexual relationships. The males would typically indulge in more exploratory behaviour than the females, par-

A macaque monkey at the Japan Monkey Centre at Inuyama reveals a talent and liking for bipedal locomotion. Opposite: another macaque at the Centre plunges into the sea to join others apparently bathing for pleasure

ticularly in search of food. All-male foraging groups are found in chimps, for example. Facial expressions, vocalizations, postures and gestures would be complex and in many ways 'man-like'. Like the pongids, early hominids probably built nests, sometimes used tools, and used objects in intimidation displays. Finally, a point I have mentioned before, they probably approached problem-solving not by a process of trial and error, but rather by hypothesis-making and -testing. Ecologically, these earliest hominids would probably have been mostly forest forms. But at some stage the ecological setting would have shifted to the forest-fringe zone close to the savannah. At the same time perhaps (though this, like much else, will be difficult to prove) their diet would have changed. All primates are vegetarians, although in some cases animal protein may often be added to the diet. If we could describe an 'average' human diet at all, we would note the relatively large amount of meat eaten. Men, at some stage, stopped being vegetarian foragers and became hunters as well as gatherers; they became in effect social carnivores, cooperative hunters.

Hominids seem to have evolved from pongids that were also ancestral to the chimpanzee and gorilla, possibly to the orang too (although probably not to the gibbon). This common ancestor would have been less specialized than both the living apes and ourselves. Soon after the hominids diverged, it is thought, they became bipedal. This change would have had quite profound behavioural and social connotations. The hominids are dentally peculiar primates and these specializations seem to be quite ancient too. Once again the distinctive hominid morphology has considerable social and behavioural implications. The order of appearance of the locomotor and dental specializations is not known. It can be – and has been – argued that they came as a package, but for the present this must remain complete speculation. What is known is that it is only long after stone tool-making traditions became established that we find the human brain growing to its present relatively great size.

Human dentition compared with that of other primates, such as the baboon (opposite) and the gorilla (below), is in many respects exceptional, most obviously for the modest size of the canines in males as well as females

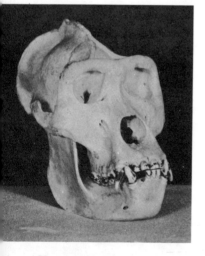

Perhaps the most obvious of man's unique features are brain size, and tooth and locomotor specializations. Humans have relatively enormous brains: on average about 1400 c.c. in volume – some *three times* the average of 400 or 500 c.c. for apes. Early hominids, or hominid ancestors, must obviously have had much smaller brains than we do now, but this of itself would not turn our ancestors into apes, unless we redefine 'ape'.

Our dentition is unique because both male and female have small canines that closely resemble incisors and do not project beyond the level of the other teeth. Compare human dentition with that of another primate – with the gorilla, for instance. First, the molars and premolars differ. In gorillas the cusps are rather pointed and projecting, probably an adaptation to chewing tough vegetable material. If we had taken the chimp as an example we would have found the molars much more human-like. (However there are many subtle ways in which human molars differ even from those of chimpanzees.) Next, in male gorillas the canines of both upper and lower jaws are long and pointed and they interlock with one another (the upper ones behind the lowers, and outside the lower premolars). Because of this projection the front lower premolars are modified and differ from the second lower premolars which are bicuspid teeth (having two cusps). The first premolars are not bicuspid but consist of one main cusp with perhaps a tiny subsidiary inner

one. The tooth crown is elongated from front to back and therefore contrasts strongly in morphology with the second premolar. The two premolars are said to be 'heteromorphic'. The elongated single-cusped front premolar shears against the large upper canine rather like blades of scissors – the premolar is therefore a cutting, or 'sectorial', tooth. Sectorial front premolars are practically universal among male primates other than man. In females the picture is somewhat different. The upper canine is small and barely projects beyond the tooth row. The front lower premolar is less elongated than in males, although it is still not a completely bicuspid tooth like the one behind it. Obviously this canine/premolar grouping is a functional complex. If the upper canine is reduced the lower premolars will tend to resemble each other. In hominids this has proceeded much further than in female apes and both the lower premolars are bicuspid and practically identical. They are said to be 'homomorphic'.

What are the functions of the big canine in male primates? Although having such a tooth is obviously going to be useful in some feeding behaviour, this cannot be the main reason for its purpose because males and females feed in the same ways on the same foods, and females have small canines. So the answer must lie in something that males do and females do not. Male primates use their huge canines in asserting dominance and in aggressive displays. They rarely use them in actual physical fighting, but do use them for intimidation. Now, looking at the human dentition we can see that males have relatively tiny canines, just like females. Why should this be? Probably because inter-individual behaviour in humans – particularly between males – differs from that among non-human primates. When we look at primitive hunter-gatherer society we can see that although males are broadly speaking dominant to females, because of their economic role, there are no dominance relationships in the way there are in baboon or gorilla society. As E. R. Service puts it:

'Hunting-gathering bands differ more completely from the apes in this matter of dominance than do

any other kinds of human society. There is no peck-order based on physical dominance at all, nor is there any superior-inferior ordering based on other sources of power such as wealth, hereditary classes, military or political office. The only consistent sup-remacy of any kind is that of a person of greater age and wisdom who might lead a ceremony.

'Even when individuals possess greater status or prestige than others, the manifestation of the high status and the prerogatives are the opposite of ape-like dominance. Generosity and modesty are required of persons of high status in primitive society, and the rewards they receive are merely the love or attentive-ness of others. A man, for example, might be stronger, faster, braver, and more intelligent than any other member of the band. Will he have higher status than the others? Not necessarily. Prestige will be accorded him only if these qualities are put to work in the service of the group – in hunting, let us say – and if he therefore produces more game to give away, and if he does it properly, modestly.'

An all-male gathering in Arnhem Land, at which newly initiated Aborigines are being shown certain marked stones considered too sacred to be seen by women

Co-operation in the hunt and in the sharing of food is one of the bases of human society. Above: a group of bushmen in Botswana butcher a gemsbok which the men have just tracked and killed

Generosity, cooperation, and reciprocity tend to be the norm, and it is fairly easy to see why. Without the most intense cooperation between males in hunting and also between whole families in food-sharing, this type of society would cease to exist. Yet it existed for upwards of 2 million years. Disruptive incidents must have been kept to a minimum, and the potentially dangerous male aggression checked and controlled. This was accomplished in a whole series of complex cultural and behavioural changes.

There remains the problem of explaining exactly how the canine became reduced, because genetical theory almost demands that there be positive selection for a morphological change in order to produce the change. The shrinking could be an indirect consequence of hormonal alterations, but this is very unlikely. Professor G. Evelyn Hutchinson has suggested that reduced human canines appeared when humans lost their hairy coat, so that injuries during play (and fighting) could be avoided; an intriguing suggestion and one which should be considered in more detail.

When human males do fight, they do so not with teeth, and generally not with fists either, but with weapons; and of course weapons are necessary for the hunt. It has become practically a matter of anthropological dogma (one to which I have always subscribed) that reduced canines and weapons–replacement canines–go together. Even so, why not keep big canines as well as have weapons? Because, according to Hutchinson's idea, canines became small to avoid damage to hominids from any fighting within the troop. Canine reduction may also be associated with the improved slicing and cutting ability of hominid front teeth, and this is perhaps the more convincing reason.

Moving forward in the tooth row to the incisors, we note that in man they are relatively small, at least compared with those of the chimpanzee or the gorilla. In chimps and gorillas the incisors are enormous. I have already suggested that this must have something to do with feeding behaviour. The earlier dryopithecines and most monkeys have quite small incisors, so the human condition may be in part a primitive survival. Small incisors in early man indicate that feeding behaviour was not as it is in living apes. Either the food eaten did not require large front teeth or–probably less likely–food was being prepared in some fashion before being eaten.

With a combination of small canines that look like incisors, and small incisors themselves, the human dentition is relatively short from front to back. This has affected the shape of the tooth row so that instead of being shaped like an inverted U (with parallel sides), it is parabolic (steadily widening towards the back). The total morphological pattern (to use Sir Wilfrid Le Gros Clark's phrase) of the dentition is quite distinctive. Not just one feature but the whole complex of features is what counts.

Bipedalism

The skull of a modern man consists of a rounded braincase which surrounds and protects the brain and provides attachment for muscles, particularly those

Typical dental arcades in modern man (top) and the chimpanzee. In the latter, the molar rows are virtually parallel; in man they curve towards each other and are relatively farther apart

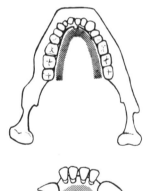

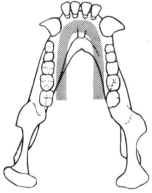

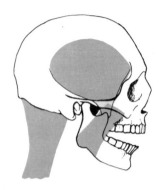

The positions of the nuchal (neck) and main chewing muscles. Below: simplified hind view of the skulls of a gorilla (top) and man, showing the relative area of attachment of the nuchal muscles (1), and the positions of the occipital condyles (2) and the foramen magnum (3). In man the foramen magnum is too far forward to be seen

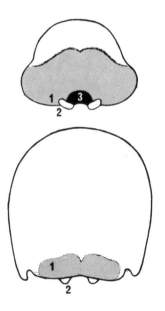

used in chewing. The braincase sits behind and on top of the face, the form of which is determined by the size of the teeth (and hence the jaws) and the size of the nose region. In man the jaws are small and the face relatively flat (although the bones at the top of the nose are left sticking out on their own) and tucked in under the braincase. The skull is nicely balanced on the vertebral column. The foramen magnum (the hole through which the spinal cord passes into the skull) is placed relatively far forward, and the area for the attachment of the neck (or nuchal) muscles is small and is directed more or less downwards. If the head is well balanced, and if they are not required in fighting, neck muscles can be small. Male primates generally need to balance and move rapidly their large faces and big, projecting canines. Men do not need to do this. The foramen magnum also faces more or less directly downward in man, not relatively backwards as in apes. In modern *Homo sapiens* the braincase is short and high and the brain overlaps the orbits. This results in a high, vaulted frontal region lacking prominent brow ridges, and a fairly evenly rounded occipital region.

The human adaptations for habitual erect bipedalism – walking involving full extension of the hip and knee and final pushing-off just from the big toe (what Dr John Napier has succinctly termed 'striding')–are widespread. The presence or absence of bipedalism in fossil men is easily detectable, given the right fossil bone.

The human vertebral column is arranged–in the living species–to form a series of curves. The one which concerns us here is the lumbar curve, a forward convexity in the region of the pelvis and lower back. Its function is to improve body balance in the upright position. The curve is formed by the shape of the intervertebral discs and also by the shape of the vertebral bodies themselves. Thus lumbar and sacral vertebrae in the lower back of men are longer at the front than behind. They are therefore wedge-shaped in side view.

The pelvis in man is broad, shallow from top to bottom, and bowl shaped. It is adapted for supporting abdominal organs; for giving attachment to abdominal muscles and also the muscles that move the legs and control the posture of the trunk on the legs; for passing a large-brained infant (only in females); as well as for a number of other reasons. The short and broad shape of the human pelvis, and particularly the iliac bones, is quite distinctive.

If we look at the skeleton the heads of the femora – the thigh bones–are relatively far apart, while the lower ends are close together. Both ends have certain features that are distinctively hominid, though only a couple need be mentioned here. With the knees together, the top of each tibia–shank bone–is horizontal and so too are the bottoms of the femora. Yet the two femur shafts diverge outwards and upwards towards the hips and form an angle to the vertical. This angle is called the 'carrying angle'. The angle is present so that with each step the axis of weight transmission in the lower leg and foot remains close to the central axis of the body and hence to its centre of gravity. Weight transmission still tends to fall through the outside of the femur, however, and the outer condyle of the femur is therefore larger than the inner. (In apes the reverse is true.) Broad hips and carrying angle mean that the femora form two sides of an inverted triangle. This arrangement greatly improves stability in walking for with each step the pelvis, together with the rest of the body, can be rotated round the axis of the fixed tibia and foot, while each footstep follows a more or less straight line. Muscles connecting pelvis and femur contract and cause the pelvis to rotate on the leg. These movements are performed with maximum efficiency because of the various bony and muscular adaptations.

Perhaps the most distinctive adaptation to bipedalism is found in the structures of the foot. First, the toes are short, a characteristic of the feet of all terrestrial primates, and the tarsus is relatively long. The metatarsals are parallel, and the first lies alongside the second and articulates with it at their bases. In all other primates the great toe diverges and can be moved to and fro and used in grasping. The tarsal and metatarsal bones of man are so shaped that they form two arches, one

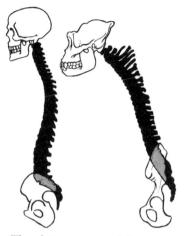

The relative curvature of the vertebral column and position of the skull in man (left) and the gorilla. In man the skull almost balances on the vertebral column; in the gorilla virtually the entire weight of the skull is concentrated in front of it

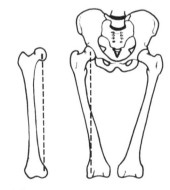

The carrying angles and direction of weight transmission of the femora of the gorilla (left) and man. The relatively large carrying angle in man greatly improves bipedal stability

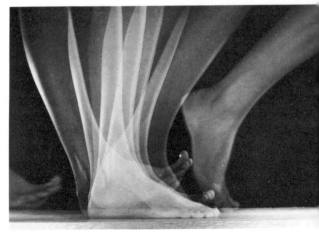

Above right: the planting and raising of the foot in normal human bipedal locomotion, and (above) diagram of the essential skeletal and muscular elements involved

running from front to back, the other from side to side. In this way the foot behaves like a spring under tension. Weight is transmitted through the arches, down the outside of the foot, through the heads of the metatarsals, and finally to the great toe. At the final moment of striding, the weight of the body is propelled by the tip of the great toe alone. In man the first and fifth metatarsals are the most robust, reflecting the pattern of weight transmission, and the last segment of the great toe is very distinctive – all reflections of the unique function of the foot. Even an isolated last segment of great toe (or distal phalange, in technical language) can indicate whether or not an animal was a biped.

Bipedalism and the hand

What about the origins of bipedalism, a problem which has puzzled anthropologists for a long time? Unfortunately, bipedalism is a unique locomotor phenomenon among mammals, so there is no comparative material. However, almost all living primates are bipedal from time to time. Vertical clingers and leapers spend most of their time resting and leaping with their trunks erect. When they move to the ground they become upright bipedal hoppers, using their powerful hind-limbs to progress in frog-like leaps. So there is here a possible preadaptation for human bipedalism. It is quite improbable that we did not have a quadrupedal phase in our ancestry, so we would not have gone straight from vertical clinging and leaping to bi-pedalism. Turning therefore to quadrupedal monkeys, again it is possible to find animals that have powerful hind-limbs for leaping, that often keep the trunk erect while sleeping and feeding, and that often stand erect while carrying objects and also while scanning the countryside for predators.

Among the hominoids, gibbons keep their trunks erect for brachiation and the animal often walks bi-pedally along branches. The other apes are bipedal too in a variety of circumstances. Like monkeys, they may be bipedal when carrying objects–food, for example. They are also bipedal during agonistic displays, and this is perhaps the most important aspect of their bipedalism. With a bit of juggling it is possible to persuade wild-reared chimps under naturalistic zoo conditions to charge bipedally and throw branches at predators (leopards). Under wild conditions chimps, orangs, and gorillas will hurl branches, stones and lumps of earth when they are excited, either angry or simply pleased to see each other.

The combination of circumstances which led to the emergence of hominid bipedalism two million or more years ago was clearly unique, yet once established bipedalism was extremely successful. There was pro-bably a whole complex of selection pressures: for making oneself look bigger and more intimidating; for object-carrying (food or babies); for weapon-use (stabbing, clubbing or throwing); and to increase visibility. Once evolved, bipedalism becomes an effi-cient means of covering the large distances necessary in hunting. So this could be another factor too. One can see here a relationship between tool-use and bipedalism, though whether this is really a causal relationship as some (including myself) have stated, must remain more than a little doubtful. Anthropologists are very fond of the phrase 'the emancipation of the fore-limb' as an explanation of the relationship between tool-use and bipedalism. But what kind of tools? Tools for digging

Even so specialized an arm-swinger as the gibbon may frequently resort to walking on two legs

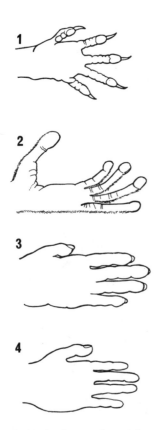

The hands of a tree shrew (1), an indris (2), a chimpanzee (3), and a man (4). In man the ability to oppose thumb and fingers with both firmness and delicate precision is more highly developed than in any other primate

roots, cutting meat, or smashing bone, are used mostly sitting down. They do have to be carried, but they could (just) be carried by a quadruped. But weapons—tools used for hunting and fighting—can generally be used only from an upright position. Only in this sense is the fore-limb emancipated by the adoption of bipedalism.

There are a few more points to be made about human anatomy, particularly the chest, upper arm and hand. The chest is broad and shallow, the collar-bone is long, and the shoulder blades lie on the back rather than the sides of the chest as in quadrupeds. All these are resemblances to other hominoids and are thought to be associated with brachiation. They have therefore been taken as evidence of a brachiating ancestry in our past. But this view only holds if all living non-human hominoids were in fact brachiators—and I have shown that this is not really the case. The view is also rather anti-evolutionary and decidedly non-functional, and assumes that structural features remain unchanged when put to different uses. The shape of the chest can be explained in functional terms since, if an animal is upright, a broad shallow chest is easier for balancing the body than a narrow deep chest would be. There are likely to be other reasons too (muscle origins, perhaps) but this seems plausible enough. It is interesting to note that vertical clingers and leapers also combine broad chests with erect trunks. The shape of the shoulder blade and the structure of the upper arm are also supposed to be features specially relating man to other hominids. But a recent detailed and elegant statistical study (using many characters rather than one, hence termed a 'multivariate analysis') has shown that human morphology is completely different from that of all other primates; it combines selection for mobility with well developed arm-raising muscles and relatively weak propulsive muscles. Selection for throwing, as well as for general hand and arm mobility, would achieve this end result.

The human hand differs structurally and functionally from that of all other primates. With hands we make the tools so necessary for our survival. Ours is a fairly typical terrestrial primate hand with five rather straight and relatively short digits. But the thumb is relatively long compared with the other fingers, and its muscles and ligaments allow it a tremendous range of mobility. The human hand can be used not only for powerful gripping of objects but also for fine manipulative work. Such delicate work is made possible partly because of the proportions of the fingers and the mobility of the thumb; the sensitive thumb pulp pad can be opposed to the pulps of all other fingers, something other primates cannot do. But hand use depends on other factors too. First, it depends on the ability to control movements not just of the hand but of the forearm and upper arm as well. Thus accurate striking involves power and control. Most important of all, the hand must be wired to the proper sort of brain. Intricate relationships between the cerebrum and the cerebellum in the brain are responsible for the fine control of all movements. The human cerebellum, like the cerebrum, is much larger than in apes. Exquisite visual, tactile and motor coordination are needed to achieve the fine movements of human hands, and it is not easy to infer merely from hand proportions, say, the functional capabilities of hands. In much the same way, we speak not so much because we have a human tongue and larynx but because we possess a human brain built for speech.

The hands and feet of the chimpanzee are almost equally prehensile, but neither can match the fine control associated with human hands

Until very recently it was believed that the hominid fossil record only began in the Pleistocene. Now the situation is rather different and it is quite likely that Tertiary hominids did exist, although this view is not universally accepted.

Before turning to the hominids, however, we must consider an animal that is almost certainly not a hominid, but which was at one time thought to be. This is *Oreopithecus bambalii*, first found in Tuscany during the last century. *Oreopithecus* has had quite a chequered history and has been described as monkey, ape, hominid and even pig! The dentition and jaws were the first parts to be found and, together with a few limb bones, remained the only parts known until 1958 when a complete skeleton was found in a Tuscan lignite mine. A detailed study of the teeth and skull shows that the brain size was bigger than that of monkeys and was within the range for chimps. The skull was quite delicately rounded, the face almost flat and not projecting as in living apes, the chin region vertical, the incisors and canines small, and the relative proportions of the teeth hominid-like rather than pongid-like. It was suggested therefore that *Oreopithecus* was a human ancestor. So-called hominid features were also found in the skeleton. Later, a detailed study of the dentition showed that in a number of very important features *Oreopithecus* differed markedly from

Opposite: the almost complete, though considerably distorted, skeleton of Oreopithecus, from early Pliocene deposits in Italy. Detailed study indicates that it is an aberrant ape and not ancestral to man, as was at first surmised

Skull of Apidium, a catarrhine primate from Oligocene times which bears a close resemblance to Oreopithecus

the hominids. For one thing, cheek teeth had a completely different morphology, and the canines and incisors when examined very carefully also proved to be quite distinctive and unlike those of hominids. Rather, *Oreopithecus* resembled a catarrhine primate, *Apidium*, from the Oligocene Fayum deposits of Egypt. Among primates, *Oreopithecus* and *Apidium* are unique in sharing a number of specialized dental features not found elsewhere, and this may imply some kind of evolutionary relationship between them. *Apidium* was a small, short-faced primate looking not unlike a South American marmoset and it seems to have been a vertical clinger and leaper. Most workers now accept the idea that *Oreopithecus*, and perhaps *Apidium* as well, should be classified not within the Hominoidea, but in a new family, the Oreopithecidae.

Both *Oreopithecus* and *Apidium* were very short-faced forms with small canines. Both these features are found in hominids of the genus *Homo* and this is what produced the confusion. It has now become clear however that for some hominoids short faces and small canines are merely primitive features, and not inevitable pointers to hominid ties. Actually the canines of male *Oreopithecus* specimens are not particularly small, being only a little smaller than those of some male chimps. Detailed study of the post-cranial skeleton shows that in spite of some claims to the contrary *Oreopithecus* was not a biped. The arms were longer than the legs, hands were long and curved, and all joints, including hip and ankle joints, were adapted for mobility. This indicates that *Oreopithecus* was either an arm-swinger or a quadrumanous climber.

The Ramapithecus controversy

We shall now turn to a form which is considered by some to be a very plausible pre-Pleistocene human ancestor. In 1934 G. Edward Lewis, a Yale research student, went on an expedition to the Siwalik Hills of northwestern India. The geological deposits there run in age from middle Miocene right through to the present day, but Lewis found what he was looking for –

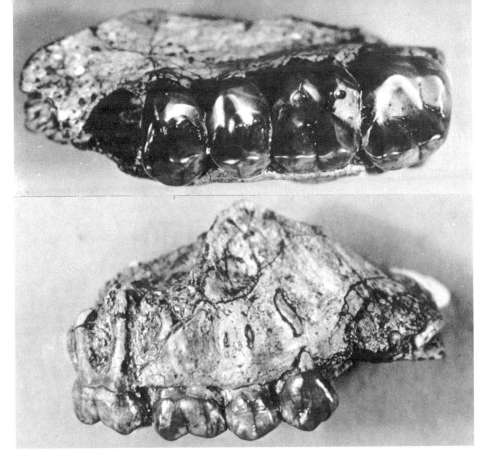

primates—in late Miocene and early Pliocene beds. The absolute age of these we have to guess at since there are no rocks suitable for absolute dates, but they are probably between about 14 million and 8 million years old. The pongids that he discovered have already been discussed. They belong to *Dryopithecus* and some of them may be ancestral to the orang utan.

Among his collection of primates Lewis found pieces of upper and lower jaws which he thought looked rather man-like. None of the finds had upper and lower jaws associated together and, after the fashion of the times, Lewis proceeded cautiously and described the upper jaw fragments as *Ramapithecus* and the lowers as *Bramapithecus*. Taking first the upper jaws Lewis made a new species, *Ramapithecus brevirostris*, based on a single piece of bone with two molars, two premolars,

Upper-jaw fragment of Ramapithecus, the earliest known man-like primate, thought by some to lie in the direct line of human descent

the canine socket, an incisor root, and part of the socket for the central incisor. The cheek teeth were approximately the size of those from a female chimp, while sockets and root showed that the front teeth were relatively very small indeed. The face had been quite short, and the part below the nose hardly projected at all (hence the name '*brevirostris*' – 'short-snouted'). Lewis noted that in combination these characters were man-like rather than ape-like and so he thought that *Ramapithecus* was either a 'progressive' pongid or a very early hominid.

This was a startlingly advanced view for the 1930s. In those days a fossil had to be practically identical to *Homo sapiens* to qualify as a hominid! Unfortunately Lewis was a young man and few people took much notice of his paper, although he had discussed his find with eminent palaeontologists like W. K. Gregory. To cap it all the senior physical anthropologist at the Smithsonian Institution, Ales Hrdlička, examined *Ramapithecus* and pronounced it a man-like 'progressive' ape; not a hominid. Hdrlička was an extremely able anatomist and physical anthropologist, but fossil primates were not his *forte*. In this case he made a mistake, and made it in a rather unnecessarily polemical way. Hrdlička asserted, however, that *Ramapithecus*, although clearly not a hominid, was nevertheless more man-like than *Australopithecus*, now almost universally accepted as a hominid.

Much of the trouble stemmed from the definition of 'hominid'. Today we would define the family to include living men and their fossil ancestors back to the time of divergence from proto-apes, or at least far enough back to be able to detect hominid features. When Lewis wrote his 1934 note he was cautious and went along with the consensus view as to what a hominid was. Later in his unpublished doctoral thesis he went much further and described *Ramapithecus* as a hominid ancestral to *Australopithecus* and *Homo*. In the Peabody Museum at Yale University there is a chart designed by Lewis showing human ancestry back into the Miocene. The chart was prepared in 1940 and agrees in essential details with much of today's consensus. Lewis was remarkably perceptive.

Unknown to Lewis, perhaps because he never personally examined the fragment, another piece of *Ramapithecus* upper jaw had been found much earlier, in 1915, and had been called *Dryopithecus punjabicus*. The piece contained two molars and both premolars, plus part of the canine socket showing that the canine was tiny. In all essential features this specimen and *Ramapithecus brevirostris* are the same; that is to say, they differ no more than would any two individuals drawn at random from the same species. This palatal fragment, *D. punjabicus*, has caused a great deal of trouble for workers. Upper jaws of Eurasian *Dryopithecus* are exceedingly uncommon, and this supposed *Dryopithecus* was well preserved and relatively complete. It therefore became the yardstick against which all new fossil apes were compared. Thus when the species of *D. (Proconsul)* were first being described, the palate from India was used as comparative material (as the describers believed) of *Dryopithecus*. Not surprisingly, *D. (Proconsul)* differed from this '*Dryopithecus*', which was in fact a *Ramapithecus*.

In 1961 Professor Simons published a short note which drew attention to the hominid features of *Ramapithecus*, and gave some reasons for believing that the tooth row had been parabolic rather than U-shaped. By this time people were not so averse to the idea of pre-Pleistocene hominids. With the acceptance of *Australopithecus* as an early Pleistocene human ancestor, it seemed fairly clear that there must be more still further back in time. Nevertheless, since the 1930s *Ramapithecus* has always been described along with the dryopithecines. As I have already said, the dryopithecines were thought to be remarkably prolific of species, splitting and branching out very many times. Some of these were thought of as more or less man-like, although exactly which was closest to human ancestry was always a bit puzzling. *Ramapithecus* was described as man-like, but generally was considered too fragmentary for much more to be said. Altogether, the

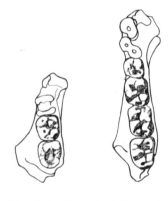

Mandibular (lower-jaw) fragments of Ramapithecus (left) and Dryopithecus. The former, which begins to curve inwards at the level of the first molar, is hominid in this respect; the latter, which does not begin to curve until the second molar, is clearly pongid

whole 'dryopithecine' complex was rather confusing. During the early 1960s, Professor Simons and I began (at first separately and later together) a revision of these forms. By 1965 we had sorted out the pongids to our satisfaction (although not to our satisfaction now!) and had separated from the apes the *Ramapithecus* upper jaws, together with lower jaws which had been placed in *D. punjabicus* with the 1915 fragment. These were all clearly man-like, looked as though they belonged to one species, and we thought that they definitely should be called hominids. We also had a close look at the mandibles which Lewis had assigned to *Bramapithecus*. Like the uppers, the lower teeth were crowded together and towards the front the jawbone curved inwards rather abruptly, both features suggesting a short-faced form. The molars themselves, and the jawbone too, were extraordinarily similar to a Pleistocene fossil hominid from South Africa (called originally *Telanthropus*, to be discussed later).

We therefore had a set of man-like upper jaws in one genus and a set of man-like lowers in another. It would be illogical in the extreme to believe that all the uppers belonged to one species while the lowers had conveniently been sampled from another. The upper and lower teeth fitted together well, and we concluded that we were in fact dealing with but a single species. This species is a *Ramapithecus*, but because '*D. punjabicus*' was named before '*brevirostris*', the correct name for the fossil species is *Ramapithecus punjabicus*. Although none of the bits assigned to *R. punjabicus* is complete, they are nevertheless extensive enough to provide a coherent picture.

Ramapithecus reconsidered

I have been very fortunate in being able to see almost all of the original specimens, and casts and photographs of the remainder. Starting with the upper jaws, let me summarize what is known. Certain features of *Ramapithecus* contrast quite strongly with those in all *Dryopithecus* species. The upper molars and premolars resemble, in a number of ways, those of *Australopithecus*,

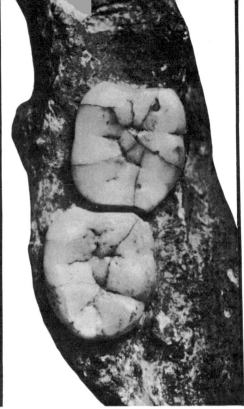

although they are not nearly as big. It is very difficult to assess adequately and quantitatively the shape of a complex structure like a molar tooth crown, and no matter how many measurements and statistical comparisons are performed one is constantly aware of this. Nowadays, however, with computers available and with the development of automatic scanning devices, it should eventually prove possible to analyse quantitatively tooth shape and so to compare one species with another in almost infinite detail. *Ramapithecus* does look in ways like *Australopithecus* in cheek and tooth structure, but there are differences and many of these can be explained as being primitive features in *Ramapithecus*. The third molar was small in some specimens of *Ramapithecus* and this has been claimed as a hominid trait, but it turns up quite frequently in Tertiary primates, also does not invariably occur in Pleistocene hominids, and anyway is subject to much variation.

Mandibular fragments of Ramapithecus (left) and a Pleistocene hominid

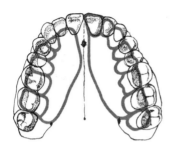

The dental arcade of Ramapithecus, superimposed for comparison upon that of modern man

Canine crowns are unknown for Indian specimens of *Ramapithecus*, but the root shape can be determined easily from the sockets preserved. Canines were small, and the roots were compressed from front to back, as in hominids, and not from side to side as in apes. Crown shape can be inferred and it is more probable than not (one is forced to be a little imprecise!) that it was like that of later hominids. There may have been a small gap between canine and incisors suggesting possibly that the lower canine projected a little, but this feature does turn up occasionally in living and fossil men so we cannot at present assess its importance. The outside, or lateral, incisor root was extremely small and so the crown must have been too. The root slopes forwards at a slight angle, but not as sharply as in living apes (although it does not differ very greatly from fossil apes). The central incisor root is known only from part of its socket. It was small, not much larger than the lateral, and curved. The root was somewhat sloping, but the crown would have been more nearly vertical.

The shape of the arcade is not certainly known but was, most probably, parabolic. This of course would be a reflection of small canines and a relatively short face. The tooth row is quite compressed, again reflecting a short face. As we have seen from *Oreopithecus*, a non-projecting facial region and small canines do not inevitably point to hominid affinities. But given the morphological features of the tooth crowns, plus other pieces of evidence, we can infer that the similarities of *Ramapithecus* to later hominids are probably homologies, due to common ancestry. In the palate therefore there is a suggestive combination of primitive and advanced features. Many of the more primitive characters are found at the front of the jaws, indicating perhaps that certain aspects of feeding behaviour were not so very different from those of other early hominoids. Yet here one is very conscious of the fact that the interrelationship between teeth and their function in men and other living primates is not fully understood, and until we do understand it we cannot really hope to interpret our fossils properly.

The handful of *Ramapithecus* fragments known so far have small canines arranged apparently as in all hominids. This implies, as noted in the previous chapter, that hominid aggressive behaviour and social structure differed in various subtle ways from that of living and probably extinct apes. It is tempting to infer that *Ramapithecus* was using tools to 'compensate' for its small canines. But apes use tools and have large canines and other primates with small canines do not use tools. Yet, might it not be argued here that because this is a hominid, the small canines are significant? I think the best thing to do is simply to state that there may be a relationship here between small canines and weapons, but it is one that cannot at present be demonstrated.

The lower jaws of *Ramapithecus* are known only partially. The molars are all approximately equal in size, contrasting with all known fossil apes and many living ones (where the third molar is bigger than the second, which is in turn larger than the first). The teeth are also compressed against one another. Both features seem again to indicate a short face, as does the curve of the jawbone towards the front. The morphology of the molars is hominid although with some reminders of more primitive relationships.

When reconstructed, the face of *Ramapithecus* looks something like that of a very short-faced pygmy chimpanzee, although of course with smaller canines and more human-like cheek teeth. What about body size? Unfortunately we have no post-cranial bones of *Ramapithecus*, so it is impossible to say anything directly about weight or stature. The cheek teeth of *Ramapithecus* are of about the same size as those of a chimp, but though *Australopithecus* had huge cheek teeth his body was lighter than that of any living ape. These contrasts may be due to dietary differences, but have never been examined. I should estimate however that *Ramapithecus* had a body size smaller than that of both *Pan* and *Australopithecus*, although how much smaller cannot be said.

Locomotion, like body size, cannot be inferred without some post-cranial bones. It would be very unwise

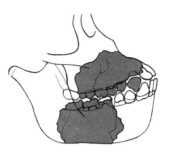

Reconstruction from discovered fragments (shaded areas) of the upper and lower jaws of Ramapithecus punjabicus

to speculate about *Ramapithecus'* locomotion from a knowledge solely of its jaws and teeth! All the known Miocene hominoids are quadrupeds of various sorts; Pliocene *Oreopithecus* was a brachiator. *Ramapithecus* or its ancestors may have been quadrupeds. Yet habitual bipedalism is, for a primate, a very peculiar method of locomotion and probably a type which has been attempted only once. It is possible that for millions of years hominids were just rather aberrant small-brained hominoids, so this might mean that there was something very peculiar about the animal which was the pre-biped. Possibly it was a quadruped which, for a variety of behavioural reasons, spent much of its time with its body in an erect position. But since we understand so poorly the relationships between environmental niche and locomotion, except in the grossest terms, I can produce no more than these vague generalities. This highlights the need not only for more fossils but also for more detailed work on the locomotor and feeding behaviour of primates in the wild. Professor S. L. Washburn has suggested that early hominids were knuckle-walkers. There is no fossil evidence to support this view, although it is certainly an interesting possibility.

While it can be stated that one species of early hominid lived in India sometime between 14 or 15 and 8 or 9 million years ago, there are hints that the same, or a very similar, species lived farther east and west. Similar animals were certainly living in Africa at this time. In 1961 Dr Leakey recovered a new fossil hominid from Fort Ternan in Kenya from deposits having a fauna of middle or late Miocene age, and fortunately they have been dated absolutely at 14 million years. This site is likely to correlate with the earliest primate-bearing beds in the Siwalik Hills of India. There are other faunal links between the two areas besides the primates.

Dr Leakey called his new primate *Kenyapithecus wickeri*. It consists of fragments of both sides of the upper jaw, plus one lower molar. The upper teeth preserved are the first two molars and the last premolar.

An almost complete canine belongs to this specimen although no socket is preserved; there is the possibility that an incisor, found nearby, comes from the same individual. The cheek teeth, which are compressed a little, resemble closely those of *Ramapithecus punjabicus*. The third molars would have been small. Once again the similarities between the cheek teeth and those of *Australopithecus* are quite apparent. The canine is particularly interesting, because it has the only crown known for a pre-Pleistocene hominid. The canine crown is small relative to the size of the cheek teeth, and much smaller than would be the canine of even a small female chimp. Set in the tooth row, the tip of the canine would have projected just a little beyond the tooth row. The crown comes to a point and is shaped not like that of *Australopithecus* but rather like a small female *Dryopithecus*. This suggests that the tooth had been modified from what was once a larger *Dryopithecus*-like canine. There is a small facet on the back of the crown worn by pressure from the front lower premolar which must have had a rather large outer cusp. It is unlikely though to have been a purely single-cusped, sectorial tooth. It looks, therefore, as though the canine/premolar grouping was well on the way to being hominid-like but was not completely so. The canine root is small and oval in outline, very similar to the socket of the same tooth in *Ramapithecus punjabicus* from India.

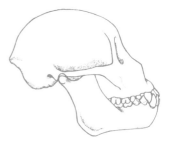

Comparison of the jaws of Dryopithecus (Proconsul) with those of Ramapithecus

In fact, in those features which can be compared, this hominid from Fort Ternan is very similar indeed to those from India, two thousand or more miles away to the east. Both Professor Simons and I have stated our belief that the African form is a *Ramapithecus punjabicus*, although Dr Leakey does not share this view. I would now think that being properly cautious we should say that the African and Indian specimens could belong to one species (which would then be wide-ranging, but no more so than *Pan troglodytes*, for example); alternatively, one could find closely related baboon or macaque species with individuals which differ no more than these hominids. In this case we could put the Fort

Ternan hominid in *Ramapithecus* but call it *Ramapithecus wickeri*. I certainly do not think that one could justify making them separate genera. Of course, even if we do put them in separate species, they are still very similar and clearly closely related to each other – like macaque or baboon species. Whether these primates belong to one species or two closely related ones, they are still very wide-ranging, and this implies that they were quite mobile, either as quadrupeds or bipeds. The Indian forms are found in deposits containing forest and woodland fauna and the climate was warm and moist. The African beds imply a similar ecological setting. Probably *Ramapithecus* was a forest and woodland form, perhaps ecologically rather like the chimpanzee and no doubt living in a variety of habitats.

With *Ramapithecus*, then, we have a plausible ancestor for the Pleistocene hominids. There is little to say about the feeding habits at present, although these may have differed in some indeterminate ways from those of apes and monkeys. The small canines are important and imply that certain basic behavioural changes had already occurred by the time of *Ramapithecus*, and these behavioural changes may have had something to do with tool- and weapon-use. Recently Dr Leakey has claimed to have found evidence which shows that *Ramapithecus* from Fort Ternan used stones at least for bone breaking. The evidence he cites is rather equivocal. The bone damage could very easily have been caused by something other than the hominids and the damage to the stone might also be due to non-hominid agencies. This sort of activity is going to be very difficult indeed to demonstrate and will require rigorous and systematic proof.

The first hominids

What about still earlier hominids? As noted in the last chapter, Dr Leakey has suggested that a primate species from earlier Miocene Kenyan deposits is a form ancestral to the Fort Ternan hominid. He calls them both 'Kenyapithecus', even though the later one so closely resembles *Ramapithecus* and the earlier one *Dryopithecus*.

There is very little reason to link the earlier and later species together as ancestors and descendants and still less to call the earlier species a hominid. Yet, if we believe that hominids are about equally related in time to chimpanzees and gorillas, then the presence in early Miocene deposits of pre-chimps and pre-gorillas implies that early hominids were in separate existence at the same time. It seems very unlikely that any known *D. (Proconsul)* species gave rise to hominids, and the other East African early Miocene species is more likely, as I have said, to be related to Eurasian *Dryopithecus* than to *Ramapithecus*. So where are the hominids? Either ancestral hominids are already known but not recognized, or they are undiscovered. I am inclined to favour the second view at present. Pehaps the sites which have been dug so far are sampling the wrong ecology for early hominids. After all, monkeys are almost as scarce in these deposits as are hominids. Perhaps early hominids had such low population densities that few of them have been fossilized.

There is an interesting but enigmatic little primate, *Propliopithecus*, from the Oligocene deposits of Egypt,

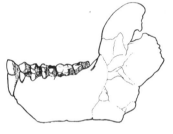

Mandible of Propliopithecus, a possible human ancestor. That Propliopithecus was an ancestor of the gibbons, as many workers have claimed, now seems improbable

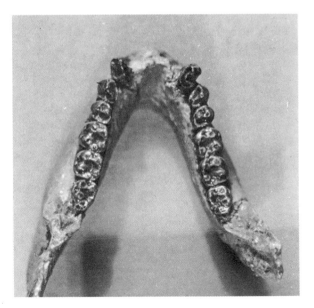

30 or more million years old. This species is known only from a couple of jawbones and a few isolated teeth. The dentition is basically very similar to that of *Aegyptopithecus*, but there are some interesting differences too. The canines are small and, although the front lower premolar is unicuspid, it is not elongated as in apes. The three molars are all of much the same size. In these features *Propliopithecus* contrasts with *Aegyptopithecus* in much the same way that *Ramapithecus* does with *Dryopithecus*. No other skeletal remains are known for *Propliopithecus*, although its tiny size suggests that it might well have been a vertical clinger and leaper like *Apidium*. In any case, the remains are too fragmentary at present to say whether this is an early hominid or not, so further discussion is postponed until more material comes to hand.

Recently two American workers, Vincent Sarich and Allan Wilson, have analyzed the albumins–blood serum proteins–of higher primates. They claim to have demonstrated, first, that the albumins in each species have evolved at a constant rate, and second, that this rate can be calculated and used to estimate the time of divergence of each lineage. They postulate that the earliest hominoid ancestral to the living species lived in Africa during the late Miocene. It was a 'brachiator' with 'brachiating' adaptations. The gibbon lineage is supposed to have split 10 million years ago, the orang 8 million, and the chimp, gorilla and man at 5 million years ago. The common ancestor of man and the African apes would be a knuckle-walker. In this way Sarich and Wilson rule out all known dryopithecines as ape ancestors and claim to explain the similarities between the various hominoids without recourse to the 'coincidence' of parallelism.

Of course parallelism is not coincidental, but is due rather to quite natural (and well understood) evolutionary processes. Moreover, as I have said, the basic hominoid similarities are nowhere nearly as marked as some have claimed; where they do exist, they are not necessarily due to exactly similar causal factors. Add to this the points that constant rates of evolution are theoretically unlikely, and that in the absence of fossil proteins it is impossible to calibrate the protein clock, and some doubts can be thrown on the theory. Finally, there is the fossil evidence; sometimes it is better not to ignore this entirely even though it is far from complete. There are quite good reasons for believing that ancestral gorillas, chimpanzees, orangs, and men were already separate 15 million years ago. Proto-gibbons are known at least 23 or 24 million years ago. If we wipe out all the fossils as ancestors of living hominoids, replacing them by unknown and entirely hypothetical ancestors for which the evidence is nil, we are erecting a scheme in which there are ancestors with no descendants along with descendants with no ancestors. Add to this the fact that if we accept this scheme we get in the late Tertiary a second radiation producing protochimps, proto-gorillas, proto-orangs, proto-gibbons and proto-men. This would be a fantastic example of parallelism, far more extraordinary than that which the Sarich and Wilson theory is supposed to explain away! One last point: how did highly arboreal gibbon and orang ancestors move across northeastern Africa, Arabia and southwestern Asia during the increasingly arid Pliocene, when a suitable habitat would almost certainly have been non-existent?

At present I think it best to say that we can trace hominids back to around 14 million years ago when they were already creatures with small canines. Before that the evidence is purely circumstantial, but I think it is possible that hominids have more ancient origins still. We can say nothing definite about their pre-bipedal locomotion. But if knuckle-walking can evolve twice in apes, as it apparently did, it might also have played some part in our own evolution, although there is some evidence suggesting that Pleistocene hominids did not have knuckle-walking ancestors.

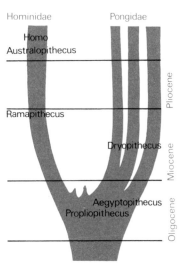

A tentative scheme of pongid and hominid evolution during the past 30 million years

THE ICE-AGE EPOCH

The Pleistocene is the most recent and consequently the best known of all the geological epochs. Rocks of this age are preserved on land throughout the world and so too are the Pleistocene sediments deposited on the ocean floor. Animals and plants, particularly for the last part of the Pleistocene, are very well known and have been used extensively to correlate one set of deposits with others in a different area. Recently methods of absolute dating of rocks have become available so that there is now a very real possibility of establishing not just relative but absolute dates for the Pleistocene. (Spot-dates do already exist, but we still lack a tight sequence of such dates–a chronology.) Since the vast majority of hominid remains comes from Pleistocene deposits, the geology of the epoch is of no small interest to us.

The Pleistocene is generally known as the epoch of ice-ages, or glacials, in temperate parts of the world; a time when great ice-sheets formed on the northern continents and spread southwards, when the polar ice thickened and spread, and when mountain glaciers descended into the valleys and out towards the plains. There were climatic fluctuations too in tropical regions, only there the changes took the form of increased effective rainfall, the so-called pluvials, rather than glacials. The fluctuations in climate in temperate and tropical regions probably ran broadly in parallel.

Opposite: a relic of the last ice age, the meandering Fiescher Glacier in the Swiss Alps

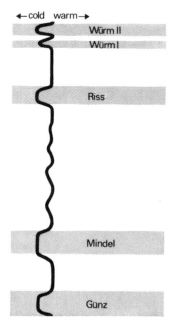

← cold   warm →

Würm II

Würm I

Riss

Mindel

Günz

The major periods of glaciation during the Pleistocene epoch

Evidence of climatic fluctuation can be found both in continental deposits (those representing environments on land: laid down by rivers, streams, lakes, deltas and buried in lavas and volcanic ashes), and in marine deposits (those laid down in the sea). The first attempts to define the onset of the Pleistocene and to break it down into time stages used continental deposits. These schemes were based mainly on the evidence for cold times left by the glaciers as they advanced, and by the presence of buried soils indicating warmer conditions. Today geological evidence is becoming increasingly diverse and depends much more on evidence from marine deposits on the sea floor.

The base of the Pleistocene has been defined in numerous ways. On geological grounds, it has been drawn at the onset of the first glaciation. This seems simple enough, except that in any given area it is never really certain that it is evidence for the very 'first' glaciation which is preserved. One particular cold period might not be equivalent to the 'first' one in some other area. Anyway, 'first' glaciations are now known to occur at very different times in different areas and perhaps this should have been expected. A glaciation reflects a climatic deterioration and climatic changes can have different effects in different places. Thus a small fall in temperature might cause certain mountain glaciers to expand – eventually leaving be-behind geological evidence of this fluctuation – while the large 'continental' glaciers might not form at all. Thus it is possible to find continental evidence of an early glaciation in the Alps, but not in England or Germany. The beginnings of the Pleistocene have been based on faunal grounds as well – being defined in terms of the presence or absence in a given area of certain land mammals, in particular *Equus* (true horses), *Bos* (cattle), and *Elephas* (elephants). There are numerous objections to this approach too. The faunas studied were originally those of western Europe. Western Europe is really only a westerly-extending peninsula of Asia and it makes a very poor reference area. (Similar objections apply to the geological subdivisions of the

Pleistocene which were also based mainly on European deposits.) Finally, these three marker genera do not in fact appear at one and the same time in Europe; *Bos* appeared first, followed by *Equus* and then by *Elephas*.

The first Pleistocene glacial scheme was based on work done in the Alps by Penck and Brückner in the early years of this century. They found evidence left by glaciers for four climatic deteriorations which they called Würm, Riss, Mindel and Günz (from youngest to oldest). The Pleistocene was thought to begin with the Günz. The colder glacial periods were separated by interglacial times when the climate was warmer, much as it is today. The time since the last glaciation has been given a special name, the Holocene, but most Pleistocene geologists would now include this in the Pleistocene. Since Penck and Brückner's work there has been a disturbing tendency to see Pleistocene sequences everywhere in terms of 'fours'. Thus, four glaciations were conveniently found in North America and numerous other places, and four pluvials turned up in East Africa. Unfortunately, the Alps are a very poor place to choose for a world-wide standard sequence. Also the glacials are known now to be not just simple events, not just a matter of ice sweeping in with lowered temperature and out again as it becomes warmer; rather they are complex fluctuations made up of numerous sub-stages. Thus the last glaciation is composed of at least two, or even three, sub-stages (or stadials, as they are known). Stadials are separated by rather warmer periods called interstadials.

The warmer times, interglacials and interstadials, are detected in a number of ways. Buried soils have already been mentioned. Deposits of interglacial age reflecting warm conditions may also be recognized by floral evidence, particularly pollen. The pollen of each species of tree or shrub is quite distinctly specific, and can be identified. It can be shown that interglacials are characterized by warmth-loving plants which during glacials are only found much further towards the equator. Each interglacial has a typical 'pollen spectrum'; the relative proportions of particular plants which remain

The relative incidence of various pollens in successive sedimentary strata reflects changing climatic conditions. Analysis of a vertical sample taken from, say, the bed of a lake (below), enables a simple chart (right) to be constructed. The relative incidence of pollens at any given time is read off horizontally

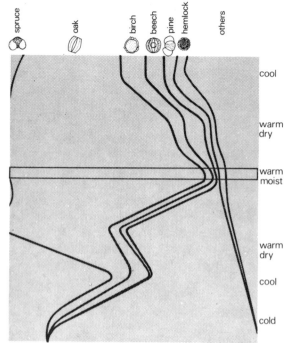

quite constant over considerable distances for a given warm period. Thus the last has a different pollen spectrum from the penultimate interglacial, and so on. So it is possible to differentiate between interglacials on this basis. Interglacials are also characterized by sea-levels higher than those during glacial periods. This is because water gets bound up in the form of ice during glacials, is thus removed from the evaporation/precipitation cycle and thereby reduces the available volume of seawater. As the ice melts at the start of interglacials, sea-level rises and 'transgressions' occur. Sea-levels will then stand high for some time and may leave evidence in the form of raised beaches. Similar structures can be found in lakes, and elevated terraces are also typical of rivers during interglacials. Different interglacials leave beaches and terraces at different levels and this evidence for raised sea-levels can be used in correlation (provided that warping and deformation of the land surface are taken into account). As the ice builds up again at the beginning of glacial times, a 'regression' of the sea occurs as sea-level falls. Interstadials differ from interglacials in being shorter and cooler and, it is thought, in showing slighter movements in sea-level.

Various attempts were made to estimate the time of onset of the Günz, and it was generally agreed that this fell somewhere between 300,000 and 600,000 years ago.

Since the 18th International Geological Congress, held in London in 1948, the base of the Pleistocene has been defined as the base of marine Calabrian deposits in southern Italy. This is the 'type' locality for the early Pleistocene. Certain changes in fauna occur near the base of these deposits; microscopic marine species previously found further north, in the Atlantic, were later found in the Mediterranean sediments. These changes were thought to indicate widespread cooling, the first cooling which was marked enough to produce detectable changes. There are problems with this definition too, of course. Some cold-loving species will

Raised beaches, as are found on the Isle of Islay (below), may indicate either upward earth movement or a fall in mean sea-level

A greatly simplified chart relating the European glacial sequence to the recently estimated dates of the onset of glaciation in other (specified) parts of the world

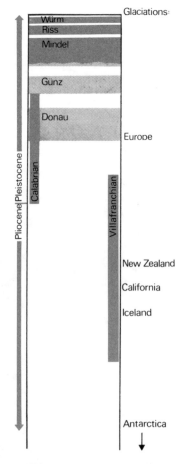

migrate before others. Some prefer to live in deep water and so are not found in deposits laid down in shallow waters near shore. Also, it could take considerable time for Atlantic elements to spread into the Mediterranean. Any boundary defined in terms of these migrations might well be 'time transgressive'. But let us ignore these objections, and accept the Congress's recommendations. Further work in Central Europe after Penck and Brückner showed that there was a glaciation preceding the Günz, and this was called the Donau. Like all the others, the Donau was a multi-stadial glaciation. The Calabrian covers pre-Günz time, and the Donau was thought to fall within this period. So, the Pleistocene could be extended backwards through time, and the generally accepted 'guesstimate' was anything up to 1 million years ago for the base of the Pleistocene drawn below the Calabrian.

The International Congress believed that the marine Calabrian was an exact time-equivalent of continental deposits covering a period of time known as the Villafranchian; the type locality of the Villafranchian is also in Italy. These marine and continental deposits (Calabrian and Villafranchian) interfinger in parts of Italy, so at least some of the sequences are time-equivalent. The Congress believed that the base of the Villafranchian was equivalent to the start of the Calabrian, so the onset of the Villafranchian came to be regarded as the base of the Pleistocene too. It is the Villafranchian which is defined by the presence of *Equus*, *Bos* and *Elephas* (although I have already said that the three genera do not in fact appear at the same time).

All this is complicated enough, and the fixing of the base of the Pleistocene is going to cause considerable trouble until we can date local sequences. We now know that each glaciation was multiple-staged, and that in any given area there may be geological evidence of many climatic deteriorations and ameliorations. The order we impose on this oscillating sequence can be, in a few cases, almost arbitrary. The problem becomes far more acute when we try to correlate one area with another. The development of methods of dating Pleistocene sediments radiometrically will eventually enable us to solve this problem in a satisfactory way. The main methods of dating are the radiocarbon (C14) method, which allows us to date back to about 60,000 years ago; the potassium/argon (K/A) method which, at least theoretically, can date rocks as young as 200,000 or 300,000 years; and some newer methods (protoactinium/thorium; thorium/uranium) which promise to fill the gaps between K/A and C 14.

Some interesting points have come from these newer dating methods. First, the time of onset of glaciation can now be dated in various areas. Thus the first glaciation in Antarctica occurred more than 4 million years ago; the first in Iceland more than 3 million; the first in California more than $2\frac{3}{4}$ million; the first in New Zealand, $2\frac{1}{2}$ million. There is evidence for very cold conditions in western Europe just under 2 million years ago although it is unlikely that widespread European glaciations occurred at this time. The Icelandic sequence is interesting for there is evidence there of at least 10 or 12 glacials and interglacials since the first.

The basal Villafranchian has been dated in Europe at more than 3 million years, and the equivalent deposits in North America give similar results. Rocks in East Africa equivalent to the start of the second half of the Villafranchian have been dated at around $1\frac{3}{4}$ to 2 million years (at Olduvai Gorge in Tanzania, an important site for fossil men). By extrapolation this would put the base of the East African 'Villafranchian' at more than 3 million years. These results caused great excitement for they seemed to indicate that the base of the Pleistocene was perhaps 3 or $3\frac{1}{2}$ million years ago. Yet this made the 'pre-glacial' (pre-Günz or Calabrian) Pleistocene incredibly long – several times as long as the rest of the Pleistocene. This certainly would apply for the Villafranchian, because detailed faunal analysis shows that a great amount of evolution occurred during this time. The faunal and floral evidence from Europe points to several fluctuations of a wet/dry type within the Villafranchian, with at least 3 or 4 complete cycles in all prior to the Günz.

Yet Calabrian deposits seemed unlikely to span this sort of time range, and a date on a pre- or early Calabrian rock had given a result of 1·6 million years. Careful stratigraphical work showed that the Calabrian and Villafranchian were not time-equivalents, and that a large part of the Villafranchian was in fact pre-Calabrian, and therefore by definition Pliocene.

Very recently, still further methods of dating rocks have been discovered. It transpires that the direction of the earth's magnetic field has reversed from time to time. Certain types of rock which crystallize from the molten state become magnetized according to the direction of the earth's field at their time of deposition. Thus in any given sequence of such rocks the direction of magnetization as one passes up through the sequence fluctuates. These reversals have been dated by the K/A method and a chronological scheme is now becoming fairly well established.

I mentioned previously that ocean floor deposits are useful in Pleistocene studies. As the microscopic organisms living in the sea die they fall to the bottom of the ocean to be deposited there along with mineral sediments. The relative numbers of different species varies with the temperature of the sea-surface waters, and for any given temperate place the fauna of a cold period differs from that of a warm period. These differences are reflected in the deep-sea deposits and a sort of layer cake of 'warm' and 'cold' alternating sediments is built up. A section of the ocean floor can be taken using a corer, a cylinder which is forced into the bottom sediments then withdrawn full of sediment. These cores are analysed for faunal changes, dated as may be possible, and palaeomagnetic reversals are determined.

The faunal changes which are believed to occur (there is a little uncertainty) at the base of the Calabrian occur also in certain North Atlantic deep-sea cores, the changes being dated by palaeomagnetic and K/A methods. These come out to around 1·8 or 1·9 million years. If the events in the North Atlantic and in the Mediterranean were contemporaneous the base of the Pleistocene is around 1·85 million years old, consider-

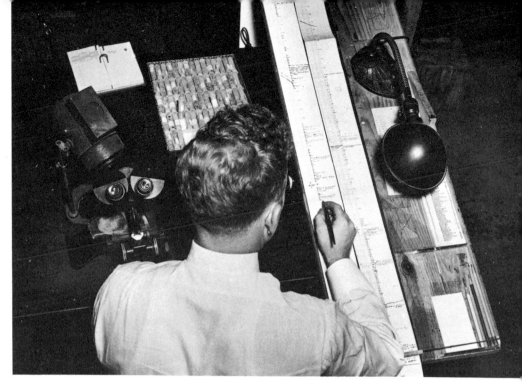

ably younger than the earliest Villafranchian. This
actually seems quite reasonable, for I have already
mentioned that evidence of cooler conditions was
found in European continental deposits somewhat less
than 2 million years ago; these cooler conditions might
be those responsible for the massive faunal shifts found
at the base of the Calabrian.

World-wide climates throughout the entire Tertiary
seem gradually to have become cooler and geological
evidence shows that the cooling reached sufficient proportions to produce glaciations in mountain regions
and in high latitudes earlier than 2 million years ago.
Just after this the cooling caused a shift in marine faunas
which is detectable in the Mediterranean, and which
defines – arbitrarily – the onset of the Pleistocene. Warm
and cool oscillations followed this, increasing in magni-
tude gradually so that cool, moist continental conditions
and small mountain glaciations gave way to widespread
continental and very extensive mountain glaciations.
The dating in Europe of the detectable glaciations, the

*A palaeontologist plots the micro-
scopic fossil content of a core of
sedimentary rock*

Rock engraving of a hippopotamus at Wadi Djerat recalls a time when water was plentiful and luxuriant vegetation covered the Sahara

classic four plus the Donau, brings us to a virtual halt because not only are there disagreements about stratigraphy but the absolute dates are often wildly at variance. Dates for the last glacial are fairly well agreed upon. World-wide climatic deterioration began around 70,000 years ago. Glacial conditions were matched by pluvials in the tropics; average rainfall increased in most places, and cooler temperatures reduced evaporation. The forests spread and in Africa almost covered the continent south of what is now the Sahara, which itself turned into savannah and woodland. Similar conditions probably obtained in earlier pluvials. This last glaciation (called Würm in the Alps, Weichsel in northern Europe, and Wisconsin in North America) was split into two main stages. The first lasted until around 45,000 or 50,000 years ago; the succeeding interstadial finished just over 30,000 years ago to be followed by very severe cold conditions. The glacial ended, after more oscillations, about 10,000 or 11,000 years ago. The climate has fluctuated since then.

The final interglacial (called variously Riss/Würm, Saale/Weichsel, Eem or Eemian) probably began about 100,000 years ago, and lasted 30,000 years. Unfortunately, at least two and perhaps three separate raised beaches of different ages have recently been found within this time period. Nevertheless, the Eemian within the European continental sequence is still best regarded as one event. Before that came the complex Riss glaciation (known in northern Europe as the Saale). This has three, possibly four, stadials, and at least one of the interstadials was quite extensive. The time of onset of the Riss is very difficult to estimate. The preceding interglacial (Mindel/Riss, Elster/Saale, or Holstein) is quite well known in Europe. Although its duration has been debated (it was once called the 'great' interglacial), it is now thought probably to be hardly longer than the Eemian. The age of the Holstein has been variously dated to about 200,000 years (which would make the Riss a long glaciation), to about 150,000 years, and to more than 400,000! At present the middle date seems more probable. Possibly the older age, which does seem to date an interglacial, applies to a pre-Mindel warm period. A short Holstein interglacial, ending around 200,000 years ago, was preceded in Europe by the Mindel 'glaciation'. This is a very mysterious segment of time and is rapidly becoming more so. It is clearly extremely complex, and is probably of very long duration indeed. Before it there are more glacials and interglacials, stadials and interstadials, including the time known as 'Günz' and 'Donau'. Various dates have been proposed for deposits which purport to be of Mindel age, dates of 400,000 years or more, but all are dubious.

The best solution at the moment seems to be to divide up the Pleistocene locally into sections – early, middle, and late – themselves further subdivisible. The early Pleistocene runs up to Günz time (whatever that is!); the middle Pleistocene includes the span of time before the Riss glaciation; and the late Pleistocene, the best known part, covers the rest. The late Pleistocene and the later part of the middle can be subdivided and glacial/interglacial terminology of some precision used. Before that it is best to talk in broad terms only, referring whenever possible to absolute dates.

The approximate dating of recent ice ages and interglacials in Europe

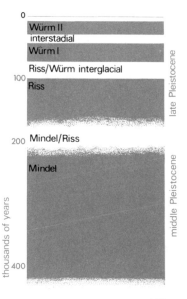

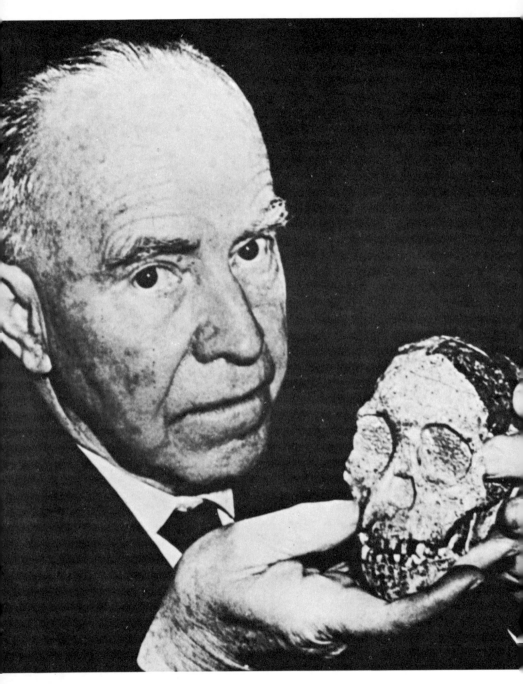

Pleistocene hominids have not been found in their correct temporal order, the earliest one first, followed by the later ones. Their recovery has been for the most part accidental and haphazard, and this has naturally affected ideas about human evolution. For example, knowledge of just the later stages of human evolution led many earlier workers to postulate certain hypothetical human ancestors. When recovered, these ancestors in fact bore little resemblance to the hypothesized forms. Early human ancestors intermediate between 'apes' and men were once thought to have big brains and ape-like jaws and teeth. Piltdown man, a supposed early Pleistocene hominid from Sussex, fitted this bill perfectly and was one of the reasons for the non-acceptance of *Australopithecus* as a hominid. *Australopithecus* had the 'wrong' combination, a small brain and man-like teeth and jaws. Piltdown has since turned out to be a fake, and the great majority of anthropologists now accept *Australopithecus* as a hominid, if not as a direct human ancestor.

Very many names have been given to individual specimens of Pleistocene hominids, and most of these are invalid either because in naming them authors have broken the rules of zoological nomenclature or because the hypothesis implied by the name is preposterous. New names do involve hypotheses, for if I find a new fossil man and give it a new species name, I imply that

Opposite: Professor Raymond Dart displays the child's skull unearthed at Taung, Botswana, in 1924. This was the first fossil relic of the hominid Australopithecus to be discovered and described

I believe that the new material is so different from *Homo sapiens* that the species represented could not normally have interbred with *H. sapiens*. If the fossils were very different from modern man, as different as *Pan* and *Pongo*, for example, I might want to put them in different genera. And so on. Even a cursory examination of fossil man shows that not more than a handful of species are required to accommodate the known material.

The most important activity for the palaeoanthropologist working with Pleistocene material is the correct temporal ordering of the fossil hominids: the oldest ones first, the youngest last, the intermediates in between. Due note is then taken of the natural variability expected of individuals within local populations and within subspecies, and of the fact that because living hominids are widespread, with several subspecies, so might be the earlier species as well. The sorts of questions to be asked are: 'Could these two fossils possibly have been drawn from one local population, or are they different enough to represent two species?', or: 'Could these two fossils from different geographical areas represent two subspecies within the same species?' Only when these questions have been answered can the fossils be organized in lineages. This is then followed by analysis and explanation of the trends within these lineages. Lastly, the lineages can be parcelled up into 'species'.

The Taung and Sterkfontein finds

In this chapter we shall discuss those fossils which are, or have been, loosely grouped as 'australopithecines'. This term implies that they are members of a subfamily Australopithecinae, distinct from less primitive hominids which would be put in another subfamily, the Hominidae. Since the differences between these two groups are not sufficient to justify subfamily division in my interpretation, I am not going to use the term 'australopithecine'.

Let us begin with *Australopithecus africanus* from South Africa, the first of this group to be discovered.

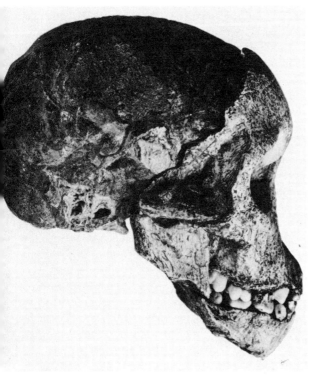

Two views of the Taung infant skull (Australopithecus africanus). Widespread scepticism was the early reaction to Dart's famous paper of 1925 asserting its man-like features. The teeth are, however, unmistakably human

This has generally been considered as an exclusively early Pleistocene species but there is a distinct possibility that at least some of its members are formally Pliocene (although still early 'Villafranchian').

The first specimen, discovered in 1924 at Taung in Botswana, was described in 1925 by Raymond Dart, then a young Professor of Anatomy at Johannesburg. Dart mentioned the many ape-like features of the skull including the small size of the brain (some 500 c.c.) and pointed to its pongid affinities; but he also emphasized the fact that there were a number of features of skull and dentition which were man-like. He proposed the new name and also suggested that the species be placed in a family intermediate between hominids and pongids. Later, when he had examined the dentition in more detail, he became convinced that *Australopithecus africanus* was a hominid. The proposal caused quite an uproar and the great majority of workers contended that *Australopithecus* was merely a man-like ape, showing interesting but irrelevant parallel features to man. (Much the same was to be said ten years later about *Ramapithecus* by Hrdlička.) Later these views were modified and many of the 'parallelisms' came to be viewed as characteristics pointing to truly hominid ties. But for some, although *Australopithecus* might be close to human ancestry, still it could not be called a hominid, mainly because of its small brain. This problem is basically a semantic one and most workers would now include in Hominidae all forms ancestral to man (or related to ancestors) back to the time when the first important features differentiated our ancestors from early apes. It is illogical to label human ancestors as 'apes', and then remove them from human ancestry because they are 'apes'!

The brain of the Taung infant had not been fossilized but there is an endocranial cast. The brain case had been filled with rock which conformed to the insides of the skull bones. Unfortunately the morphology of the inside of the skull does not repeat exactly–or even very closely–that of the outside of the brain. But there are hints that in a few ways the brain of *Australopithecus* was not completely ape-like, even though it was ape-sized. The dentition of the Taung youngster is typically hominid. The milk incisors, canines and molars are all man-like rather than ape-like, although they are larger than those of *Homo sapiens*. The mere fact of size difference is relatively unimportant. It is morphology and in particular total morphological pattern that counts far more. The permanent first molars are also human in form, but large. Because the teeth and their roots are so large, the jawbones in which they are implanted naturally tend to be rather massively built as in large-toothed apes. But the detailed morphology of both teeth and jaws is hominid.

Unfortunately the fossil site at Taung has now been destroyed by quarrying operations. The associated fauna is sparse and equivocal. Age estimates for this deposit have varied between late Pliocene and late early

Dr Robert Broom points at the skull of Plesianthropus (now transferred to the genus Australopithecus) embedded in limestone at Sterkfontein in South Africa

Pleistocene; on an absolute scale, from more than 2 million to 1 million years or less.

Just over ten years after the Taung description Robert Broom, a very distinguished South African palaeontologist, located a second hominid-bearing site in South Africa; this time quite close to Johannesburg, at Sterkfontein in the Transvaal. A reasonable sample of skulls, jaws, teeth and post-cranial material has come out of Sterkfontein, enough to allow us to infer that the material represents a fairly homogeneous population of one hominid species. This was named by Broom *Plesianthropus transvaalensis*, but has since then been transferred to *Australopithecus africanus*. It is now generally assumed that the Taung and Sterkfontein hominids are sampled from the same lineage. It is probable that the species represented would at all times have had a more extensive distribution than just Transvaal and Cape Province, although this point has generally been ignored.

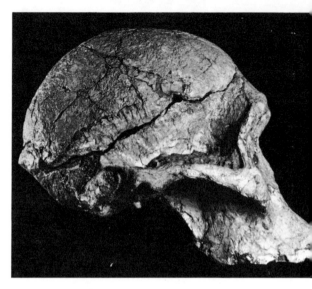

Right and opposite: two views of 'Mrs Ples', the best-preserved of Australopithecus skulls found at Sterkfontein. Below: map locating sites in Africa where fossil remains of Australopithecus have been discovered

The fauna at Sterkfontein contains many elements which unfortunately are not closely related to animals of probable Villafranchian age from other parts of Africa, so the assessment of relative age is very difficult. Neither have suitable rocks for radiometric dating been recovered from any of the South African *Australopithecus* sites. However, Sterkfontein is clearly very ancient and is at least early Pleistocene, if not older than that. The best known faunal locality in Africa of this age is Olduvai Gorge in Tanzania, some two thousand miles to the north. It is agreed that Sterkfontein is at least as old as the oldest Olduvai beds, and many workers would put it earlier still. It could be as much as $2\frac{1}{2}$ million years old, and perhaps even older.

One of the best known Sterkfontein specimens is the skull of what is thought to have been a female *Australopithecus*. The cranial capacity is around 480 c.c. and the skull is rather smoothly rounded with small brow-ridges above the eye sockets. The face is rather projecting, principally because the teeth and jaws are large, although there are other reasons too. Although 'ape-like' in its small skull and large jaws, the skull shows many contrasts with the living apes, and a number of

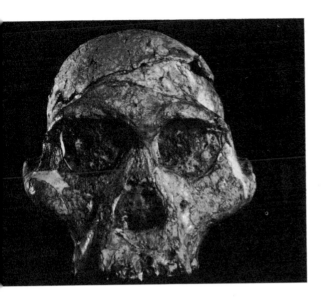

Below: hind views of the skulls of the chimpanzee (top) and Australopithecus. The much reduced area of insertion (shaded) of the nuchal muscles of the neck in Australopithecus implies an habitually vertical posture

quite detailed similarities to later hominids. At least three other skulls from Sterkfontein are well enough known to allow estimates of cranial capacity to be made. All in all, the Sterkfontein *Australopithecus* had an average cranial capacity of around 485 c.c.; close to the gorilla average of today. The four skulls actually vary in size from 435 to 530 c.c. It is possible to calculate statistically in a quite simple fashion the probable limits of skull volume in the theoretical population from which the Sterkfontein fossil sample is drawn. These limits are large. One can state, for example, that only one in a hundred of the population from which the Sterkfontein fossils are sampled would have brain volume outside the limits of 250 to 720 c.c. These limits are approximately those of the living gorilla, a species with a much greater body size than *Australopithecus africanus*. I should emphasize that it is possible that other populations of *Australopithecus africanus* from other parts of its range would have somewhat different limits.

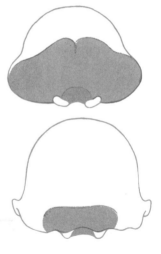

The skull shows a number of interesting features, The braincase is set rather high up, above the face. The frontal lobes of the brain surmount the eye sockets and

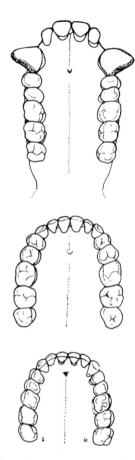

The palate and upper teeth of (top to bottom) a male gorilla, Australopithecus, and an Australian Aborigine

so the bony contour of the frontal region is arched and rounded. The brow ridges are only moderately developed. In the occipital region the skull is quite rounded, and the nuchal part of the occipital bone (where the nuchal–or neck–muscles are attached) is much more horizontal than in apes. The foramen magnum is also more horizontal. Unlike the ape condition the occipital condyles, by which the skull articulates with the spine, are set further forward. These three last points are probably correlated with the upright posture of *Australopithecus*.

The dentition is very man-like. The incisors are quite small and implanted vertically in upper and lower jaws. Morphologically, they are typically hominid as are the canines–small, spatulate teeth which barely project beyond the tooth row. The teeth are crowded together with no gaps, just as in later men, and the arcade is parabolic. The front lower premolar is bicuspid and not sectorial, and all the premolars and molars are large and relatively broad teeth. Most cheek teeth of modern man tend to be rather narrow, but some technologically primitive peoples do have broader ones, and this condition is typical of almost all middle and late Pleistocene populations, so the Sterkfontein teeth are not exceptional. The relative proportions of front and back teeth are rather as they are in *Homo sapiens*; but in overall size the teeth are big, with plenty of crushing area. As we shall see, *Australopithecus africanus* seems to have been a rather small animal and quite lightly built. Yet it was endowed with comparatively enormous cheek teeth, teeth that were bigger than those of chimps or orangs and as big as in some gorillas. All things being equal, cheek tooth size tends to be correlated with body size. Yet here is a big-toothed form with a body smaller than that of a smallish chimpanzee. Obviously all things were not equal and the important variable was probably diet. In very general terms, considering the difference in tooth size, it can be concluded that the diet of *Australopithecus* was different in some unspecified way from that of pongids.

Note that the dentition is manifestly hominid, the

only obvious difference from later men being that of size. The skull, although primitive in that it has a small brain and large jaws, is nevertheless distinctly hominid. To call *Australopithecus* an ape just because it has large jaws and a small brain is equivalent to saying that because black and white are both colours, they must be the same colour!

The skeleton of the Sterkfontein hominids is well represented. What little is known of the upper limbs recalls later hominids, though there is a hint that *Australopithecus* may have had relatively long arms. The most exciting discovery is of an almost complete vertebral column, together with most of a pelvis and the top of a thigh bone, all from a very delicately built, or gracile, biped. This particular individual was a lightly built form standing little more than 4 feet tall and weighing no more than 60 or 70 pounds. A lumbar curvature was probably present since the lumbar vertebrae appear to be wedge-shaped. The pelvis is clearly not ape-like, being short and broad like ours. From what can be seen of morphology, proportions, and muscular attachments, the pelvis was adapted quite adequately to habitual erect bipedalism. There are a few features in which the pelvis departs from the human condition and these have been interpreted as showing that *Australopithecus* was less perfectly adapted than *Homo sapiens* to upright walking; this would not really be surprising of course, although a number of these points could be explained instead by the light build of *Australopithecus africanus*. Whatever the precise locomotor behaviour of this creature, it was an habitual upright biped of sorts.

The top of the femur is interesting too in that it has a relatively long neck when compared to man. Recently Dr Alan Walker has suggested to me that this could be a means of increasing the effective stride length, important in bipedal walking; also, it would increase effective hip width, and thus improve stability in walking. Lower ends of thigh bones are also known from Sterkfontein. They show a carrying angle, and the outer condyle is larger than the inner; both of these

The pelvis of Australopithecus (top) strongly resembling in its proportions that of modern man (bottom), provides further evidence of an habitually upright posture

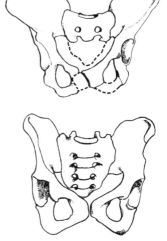

are features indicating that weight transmission was as it is in later hominids, rather than in pongids or monkeys. The lower ends also have a deep notch between the condyles which in living primates accommodates ligaments that bind thigh and shin bones together. In human walking these two bones are frequently fully extended relative to each other forming a straight line, and the ligaments then become tightly stretched to help support the knee joint. If the notch were not deep the ligaments could not tighten and perform their stabilizing function. The deep notch in the femora from Sterkfontein indicates a full extension of the knee in walking, a human trait.

When limb bones were first discovered at Sterkfontein their human form caused some workers to suggest that the bones could not possibly have come from the same species as the 'ape-like' skulls. Now there is no alternative but to assume that the primitive skulls and teeth go with the relatively advanced limb bones, a combination which has caused some surprise. But it is a generally demonstrated evolutionary phenomenon that organisms do not evolve at a given rate as a whole; rather, different parts of the body evolve at different rates. (A concept rather confusingly termed 'mosaic evolution'.)

The Sterkfontein deposit, once a cave which gradually filled with bones and other debris, was later cemented together and turned into solid rock. The *Australopithecus* fossils are found in such a way as to suggest that they accumulated in the cave at random. Individuals may have lived in or at the mouth of the cave, although this is perhaps unlikely. More probably hominids were still living in the open at this time. *Australopithecus* remains might have been taken to the cave by carnivores, or even left there by other *Australopithecus* individuals. No unequivocal stone tools have been found in the *Australopithecus* part of the cave. At this ancient time tools are sometimes difficult to recognize; if they were generally made and used in the open-air sites they might never find their way into the back of the cave. Or possibly *Australopithecus africanus* did not make regular, patterned, recognizable stone tools. It is quite probable, however, that tools of some kind were used.

With regard to stone tool-making, there are three possibilities. The Sterkfontein hominids could have lived before the invention of tool-making; they could represent a population (either as a species or subspecies) which made tools only sporadically or not at all; or the evidence of their implimental activities just might not have been discovered or recognized so far. I am slightly more inclined to favour the last hypothesis at present. Really good evidence for early Pleistocene tool-making has come from Olduvai Gorge where a combination of factors contributed to tool preservation. First, it is possible to sample at Olduvai actual living areas; and second, some of the living areas have been found complete, sealed in by volcanic rock.

The faunal and geological evidence from Sterkfontein tells us that the area looked then much as it does today: open higher country with, perhaps, wooded valleys. Streams flowed through the valleys. There was some fluctuation in rainfall during the earliest pluvials and interpluvials, varying between about half the present rainfall and half again as much. But the area would always have been relatively open country, the sort of terrain favoured by baboons or patas monkeys. *Australopithecus* therefore lived in open country. He would camp close to streams, having no method of carrying water, and probably lived in the open rather than in caves although he may have used cave mouths for shelter. There is evidence that he hunted, and hunted quite proficiently (the fact that baboons made up some of his food means that he must have been an organized, and brave, hunter). Probably each social group ranged over a wide area in search of food.

Kromdraai and Swartkrans

In 1938 a new fossil locality was found, again by Robert Broom, in the Sterkfontein valley; this time at a place called Kromdraai. Although there are some problems about the relative dating, the Kromdraai

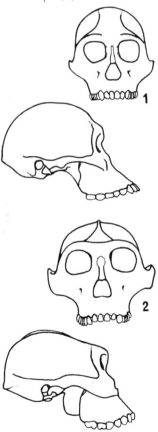

The more man-like skull of Australopithecus (1) compared with the somewhat less man-like skull of Paranthropus (2)

deposits probably fall in the middle Pleistocene. Absolute dates are difficult to estimate but somewhere between $\frac{3}{4}$ and 1 million years ago may not be far wrong. Broom thought that the new material – unfortunately he did not have a great deal of it – was so different from *A. africanus* as to constitute yet another genus and species which he called *Paranthropus robustus*. The best specimen from Kromdraai consists of part of a skull and jaws, including a quantity of the teeth. In size the teeth exceed many of those from Sterkfontein, and it is generally agreed that although the size of the front teeth remains much the same in the two samples, the Kromdraai specimen represents a population with larger molars and premolars. The skull is incomplete, but the braincase was no bigger than that of *Australopithecus africanus*, that is, around 450 to 500 c.c. in volume. Parts of the upper arm are known – the humerus and ulna from the elbow region. These have been the subject of controversy, but a recent complex statistical analysis of the humerus shows that while it is definitely not pongid, it shows some peculiarities the significance of which is poorly understood. A talus from Kromdraai came from an animal that was probably bipedal, although not as well adapted to this mode of progression as ourselves, or perhaps even as *Australopithecus* from Sterkfontein.

The climate at the time of deposition of the Kromdraai deposits was wetter than at the present day (Sterkfontein was a little drier) although this does not mean that the area was anything like forested. Although a few stone tools have been found at Kromdraai, it is almost impossible to say anything about their relationship to the fossil hominids. Rather we should turn to a site from which similar hominids are much better known.

Broom in 1949 found further remains of the same hominid at Swartkrans, closer still to Sterkfontein. His name for this form was *Paranthropus crassidens*, although it is now generally agreed that the Swartkrans and Kromdraai hominids belong to the same species, *P. robustus*. Swartkrans dates from the end of the early

Opposite top: the most-complete skull (SK 48) of Paranthropus robustus, found at Swartkrans. Bottom: the best-preserved mandible (SK 23). Both specimens are probably female

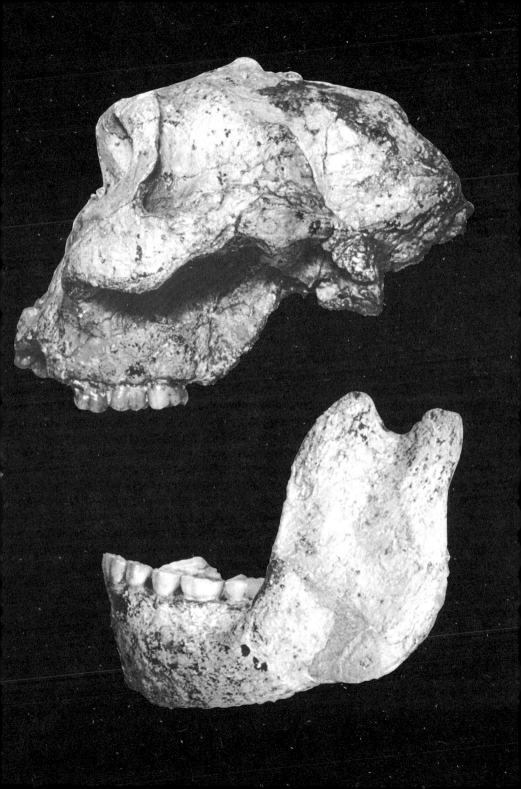

Pleistocene, or the start of the middle Pleistocene; perhaps $1\frac{1}{2}$ to 1 million years ago. (Since 1949 numerous remains have been recovered from Swartkrans and Sterkfontein, mainly due to the magnificent efforts of Dr Broom's assistant and successor Professor John Robinson. Professor Robinson has probably found more early hominids than any other palaeontologist.) The Swartkrans skulls are robust and massive. When first recovered it was claimed that 'robustus' (I shall use this term without a generic name for the moment, just for convenience) had a much larger brain than A. africanus. This is not the case, and the ranges of the volumes almost certainly overlapped. Cranial capacity cannot be calculated for Swartkrans hominids, but the average would have been in the region of 500 c.c. Compared with Sterkfontein skulls, those from Swartkrans show some interesting contrasts. The face of robustus is flatter, a little longer from top to bottom, more massive, and less projecting in the region of the teeth. The brow ridges are better developed and the forehead is almost flat rather than convex as in A. africanus. This is probably due to the fact that the braincase is set lower in relation to the face; the front parts of the brain do not overlap the eye-sockets, and so the frontal bones are not vaulted.

Turning to the dentition, we find that (just as at Kromdraai) the incisors and canines are as small as in A. africanus, if not smaller, but the cheek teeth are larger, sometimes considerably so. The molars are all big and increase in size from first to last. The back premolar in particular is large, and tends to look at times like a smaller version of the molars. It is said to be a 'molariform' tooth. What seems to have happened is this. Initially all tooth germs–tooth precursors long before eruption–have equal potential to develop into any kind of tooth. Their position in the growing jaw determines their final form; a tooth germ developing at the front will turn into an incisor or canine (depending upon its exact position), while one at the rear will eventually become a molar. It is as though there are gradients or 'fields' within the jaw, controlling the developmental future of teeth. There is a 'molar field' at the back, producing complex multicuspid teeth, and an incisor field in the front, inducing simple spatulate teeth. Intermediate fields fall between these two, and so do 'intermediate' teeth.

In *Australopithecus africanus* and *Homo* dentitions there are small but distinct breaks in morphology between canines and premolars, and between premolars and molars. In *robustus* something different happens, for the last premolar is molariform and the first is also large. There is a distinct break in size and morphology between the incisor/canine region and the premolar/molar region. The molar field seems to have spread forward changing the final form of the teeth developing within it. Although the final dentitions may show quite marked contrasts, in fact the amount of genetical change necessary to produce these morphological differences between *robustus* and *A. africanus* is quite small. Alteration of the rate and timing of growth is all that would be required.

The small anterior teeth of *robustus* contribute towards the flattened face. The large cheek teeth with their thick roots are firmly implanted in the bone of the face and lower jaws. Big chewing muscles are needed to move these, and so the entire face and associated parts of the braincase are massive and well buttressed to withstand chewing stresses. The temporal muscles, attached to the lower jaws and the upper parts of the braincase, are so large that a cranial crest is built up along the top of the skull to provide extra attachment areas for these muscles. Much has been made of the presence of this crest, another supposed ape-like feature, but it is the inevitable result of the combination of big teeth (and therefore big jaws and enlarged chewing muscles) and a small brain. If the brain grows larger so too does the braincase, muscle attachment areas can increase, and there is no need for a crest. Alternatively, teeth can grow smaller, and so can chewing muscles; a crest is also unnecessary in this case. As we have noted, the smaller-toothed *Australopithecus* from Sterkfontein lacks a crest.

A pelvic fragment (SK 50) of Paranthropus robustus, found at Swartkrans

Why should *robustus* have these larger cheek teeth? Possibly it was because of body size; so before I try to answer this let me describe some of the known skeletal material. A couple of hand bones known from Swartkrans have been studied by Dr John Napier. One he believes to be of *robustus*; the other he assigns to a more advanced hominid. According to Dr Alan Walker however both bones could belong to the same species. Little need be said about the hand from which they came, except that it was not like that of any living great ape. Part of a pelvic bone and two pieces of the femur are all that is known of the lower limbs. The pelvis shows some very peculiar features. While not ape-like it is clearly rather different from *A. africanus* as well as *H. sapiens*. The femoral fragments lead to the same conclusion. Dr Napier believes that *robustus* differed greatly from *Australopithecus* in gait, and that the two lineages possibly became bipedal independently. Other workers disagree with this view. The fossil evidence is just not adequate to test alternative hypotheses at present. Anyway, it can be said that the animal from which the pelvis came was considerably larger than *Australopithecus* from Sterkfontein. Estimates of this sort are very uncertain, but the Swartkrans hominid was probably over 5 feet tall and would probably have weighed 130 pounds or more, perhaps twice the weight of *Australopithecus*.

Studies of mammals can tell us that in subspecies or closely related species it is often the case that as body size increases so too does cheek-tooth size. As the amount of body to be fed grows bigger the amount of chewing surface also enlarges. This can be clearly seen in baboons, where males have bigger bodies, larger cheek teeth, and more projecting faces than do females. So perhaps the larger cheek teeth of *robustus* can be seen, at least in part, as related to increased body size.

The rainfall during the time of Swartkrans deposition was similar to that of Swartkrans today (less heavy than at Kromdraai), and the earlier vegetation is not likely to have differed greatly from that of today. Some stone tools have been found at Swartkrans, but

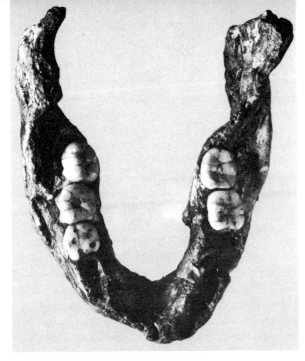

The Swartkrans mandible (SK 15)
predicated by Broom and Robinson,
of Telanthropus capensis

it is not known whether *robustus* was the maker or not because the issue is complicated by the presence of what appears to be a second hominid at Swartkrans.

In 1949 Broom and Robinson gave the name *Telanthropus capensis* to a lower jaw (mandible) from these deposits. Another jaw fragment has been recovered and also parts of the upper jaw and face, an isolated tooth, and a small piece of forearm bone. There is no geological evidence to suggest that this material comes from a later time period than the *robustus* remains, and it would be hazardous to argue, as some have done, that the two sets of specimens must be of different age because they look different! The lower jaw is much more gracile than that of *robustus*, and the teeth are smaller. It is rather broken and distorted but is probably not sampled from the same population as *robustus*; it differs a little from the Sterkfontein population too. Although the teeth were smallish, the upper jaw (maxilla) shows some features of both *robustus* and *A. africanus*.

Here, then, we have evidence that two sorts of hominids co-existed at Swartkrans. The two are related to each other but *Telanthropus* is closer to *A. africanus*, indeed it could be interpreted as a variant of this species. Robinson and others have suggested that *Telanthropus capensis* is not a valid genus and species but is in fact referable to *H. erectus*. It does show some dental resemblances to *H. erectus*, but so it does to *A. africanus*. For a variety of reasons I should prefer not to assign it to *H. erectus*, but instead to *Australopithecus*. Either *A. africanus* or *A. capensis* would do for a species name; I prefer the former at present.

It has been suggested that the tools at Swartkrans were made not by *robustus* but by *A. africanus* (or *A. capensis*) because it is more 'advanced'. This is extremely difficult to prove or disprove, but I find it hard to believe that *robustus* would not have been using tools, and probably making them as well. Perhaps anthropologists have become altogether too obsessed with tool-making. After all, there are very many activities which are specifically human apart from tool-making. One thing the Swartkrans evidence does tell us is that simple stone tool-making had begun in the Transvaal by the end of the early Pleistocene. That it had started before this is quite probable, the evidence coming not from Swartkrans but from Sterkfontein. Parts of the Sterkfontein cave deposits were thought by Robinson to be younger than the original sediments. Robinson called these areas the Extension Site (as opposed to the primary Type Site). The Sterkfontein Extension Site is thought to be somewhat older than Swartkrans. Robinson found stone tools there and a fauna which was allegedly younger than that from the Type Site. Traces of hominids have also been found and appear to be similar to the smaller hominids from Swartkrans as well as to *A. africanus* from Sterkfontein. It should be pointed out here though that there is a fair possibility that the Sterkfontein deposits are all of the same age.

Makapansgat

Let us now turn our attention to Makapansgat, a cave deposit of early Pleistocene age a couple of hundred miles to the north and east of Sterkfontein, Swartkrans

and Kromdraai. From 1948 on Raymond Dart recovered many hominids from this cave which in age
falls between Swartkrans and Sterkfontein. Its absolute
age we can estimate at between 1½ and 2 million years.
Dart first described the hominids as *Australopithecus
prometheus* because he believed they used fire. This is
now known not to be the case, and Robinson classified
the remains as *A. africanus* in his revision of the South
African early hominids. The fossils at Makapansgat
accumulated over quite a period of time, perhaps as
much as 50,000 years or more, and Dart believes that
there is evidence for climatic fluctuation during this
time. In general the climate at Makapansgat would
have been rather drier than that of the present day in
the same area.

The hominids themselves are now well known. Their
skulls were rounded just as in *Australopithecus* from
Sterkfontein. The lower jaws were also similar. The
teeth are intriguing for they seem to be somewhat
larger than those from Sterkfontein, although smaller
than the Swartkrans sample. They are variable in size
and morphology, however, and in general closer to *A.
africanus* than to *robustus*. Indeed one or two specimens
are very similar to the smaller Swartkrans hominid. As
far as the skeleton is concerned, the resemblances are in
the direction of Sterkfontein rather than Swartkrans or
Kromdraai. The pelvis is very similar to that of *A.
africanus* and shows clear evidence of adaptation to *Pelvic fragments of Australopithecus
upright walking, as well as indicating small body size.* *found at Makapansgat*

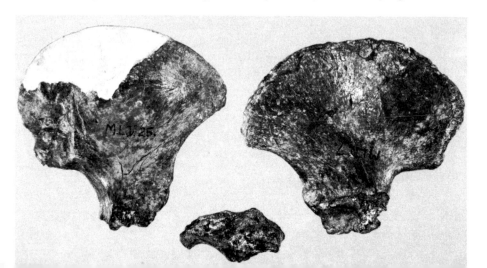

Professor Dart, who believes that Australopithecus first used animal bones as tools, brandishes a giraffe long-bone found at Makapansgat

Fragments of arm bones are said not to differ noticeably from *Homo sapiens*, although they have not yet been subjected to a detailed analysis. Professor Tobias has suggested that Makapansgat may sample a population intermediate between Sterkfontein *A. africanus* and Swartkrans *robustus*; alternatively, that it may represent a mixed, or hybridized, population. These are provocative suggestions and will require far more detailed analysis of the fossils.

Dart has claimed that he has evidence pointing to the tool-making abilities of *Australopithecus* from Makapansgat. He believes that animal bones in the deposits show clear signs of having been selected for use, brought into the cave, and utilized. Thus he sees jaws with teeth being used as knives and saws, and longbones becoming clubs. Dart's views have not been generally accepted, although it is just possible that the Makapansgat cave contains evidence of the hunting activities of *Australopithecus* and also of their implemental abilities. It is interesting to note that many of the faunal remains are small- to medium-sized mammals, or young individuals of larger beasts; large forms are often represented also by very aged animals (a hunting pattern sometimes repeated in *Homo erectus* sites). Some of the bony pieces show signs of being utilized, and even of being modified before use. There is also some equivocal evidence of stone tool use. It has been claimed that stone pounders and choppers have been found located near what was the cave mouth. It would be hard to deny that *Australopithecus* was using and quite possibly making tools at Makapansgat.

To summarize the South African material, the sites follow each other in time from latest Pliocene or earliest Pleistocene through to basal middle Pleistocene, a duration of some $1\frac{1}{2}$ to 2 million years. To extract trends or population movements, or even to make much sense out of just five scattered samples from this immense stretch of time, is going to be extremely difficult. At only one site, Swartkrans, is there evidence for two sets of hominids. Whether these are of the same species, or different species (as I believe), is arguable and one can cite eminent authorities for a variety of viewpoints. Swartkrans and Kromdraai *robustus* do seem to belong to one species, as do the Taung, Sterkfontein, Swartkrans, and Makapansgat *Australopithecus* specimens. These two groups contrast in dentition, skull form and post-cranial skeleton and many workers feel that they should be put in different genera. Although it is probable that the two groups represent different species, at present I prefer to place them, tentatively, in a single genus – *Australopithecus*. Precisely how these two groups interacted, whether they moved into and out of the fossil 'catchment areas' from different geographical regions cannot yet be determined.

Professor Robinson has proposed that *A. robustus* and *A. africanus* were adapted to different ecological niches, mainly because of differences in size of the cheek teeth. As I have mentioned, all other things being equal, increases in body size require increases in tooth size. But if the diet differs this may also alter dental requirements. If *A. robustus* were a non-tool-using vegetarian, and *A. africanus* an omnivorous hunter, Robinson argues, *A. robustus* would need plenty of tooth area for grinding its vegetable food; *A. africanus* would have a dentition proportionately similar to later hominids because its diet would resemble theirs. He supposes that scratches on *A. robustus* teeth are due to grit eaten with the vegetable food, and also draws attention to the fact that Swartkrans and Kromdraai show evidence of wet climatic conditions in contrast to the other sites. In fact the geological evidence shows that Sterkfontein was only marginally drier than Swartkrans. Anyway, even in the wettest conditions the local terrain is still likely to have been open country, not forest. Scratches appear on many *A. africanus* teeth too, and according to Professor Philip Tobias they all seem to be due not so much to grit in food but more probably to chewing on bone. However, from what we know of living hunting-gathering peoples much of their diet, in some cases up to 80 per cent, is vegetable food, so the argument is likely to be about 20 per cent of the diet! But above all, hominid dietary preferences are likely to have been flexible, much more so than in other primates. To attempt to tie a hominid down to one exclusive diet for long enough to affect morphology is, I think, asking too much. Finally, although the cheek teeth of *robustus* are bigger in area than those of *A. africanus*, they are on average only about 25 per cent greater. If the samples from various sites are used the ranges of the tooth area almost overlap, and such differences as do exist could be accounted for by differences in body size. I would conclude that Robinson has yet to produce convincing evidence for dietary differences between the South African hominids.

It is possible that several closely related populations of hominids lived in the southern part of Africa during these times, the earlier populations apparently being somewhat more 'advanced' (that is, morphologically closer to *H. sapiens*) than the later. The only evidence we have of *A. africanus* from the later part of the time range is a possible trace from Swartkrans, and this to some extent resembles the theoretical link between *A. africanus* and *H. erectus*. *A. africanus* was a creature with locomotor adaptations very much like those of later hominids. Put the right way round, this means that bipedalism is a long-standing adaptation which has been characteristic of the Hominidae for at least 2 or 3 million years. Whether it is in fact *the* basic hominid locomotor adaptation is perhaps probable, but unproven, for there are no Tertiary hominid leg bones recovered so far. The dentition of *A. africanus* was essentially human too, indicating that both social and feeding behaviour were not ape-like but man-like. How basic and long-standing these adaptations are cannot be told, although *Ramapithecus* was well on the way to acquiring them 14 million years ago. *A. africanus* was an efficient bipedal hunter living in social groupings, probably showing a division of labour between the sexes with the males hunting and the females gathering vegetable food. Cooperative behaviour would have been marked, both in hunting and in food-sharing between individuals and between

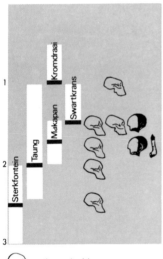

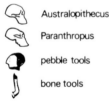

Australopithecus

Paranthropus

pebble tools

bone tools

Chronology of South African Australopithecus and Paranthropus finds. The figures indicate millions of years ago. Opposite: an imaginative reconstruction of Australopithecus africanus in his natural habitat

M.Wilson 1950

bands. Bands no doubt ranged over quite large areas and camped for days at a time at one site, generally in the open, near water, under an over-hanging cliff or near a cave mouth. Simple tools were used and made. In short, we are dealing with animals totally unlike apes in what we know of their anatomy and what we can infer about their behaviour. Although small-brained, they behaved in many ways like later hominids.

Being a mobile fair-sized hunter, *A. africanus* is likely to have been a species that ranged over considerable areas of Africa where the terrain and vegetation were suitable. In South Africa the species occupied open woodland and savannah and this was probably their usual type of territory. Men seem mostly to have avoided forests until relatively late in their history. The fossils come from a few sites in a restricted part of South Africa (and this handful of localities covers very thinly a fair time span). They represent in fact just a segment of a more widely distributed species. In all probability what we are dealing with is a sample drawn from a subspecific population rather than from a purely South African species. This has too often been forgotten in the past. The actual story of course is almost certainly much more complicated than we now suppose.

Bearing all these points in mind we now move several thousand miles to the north, to East Africa. There the story is a little more satisfying, for not only can Villafranchian-equivalent faunas be arranged in their temporal order, but there are also some absolute ages from K/A dates on suitable volcanic rocks.

Olduvai Gorge

The East African hominids can best be interpreted as belonging to two distinct lineages, each of which lasted for a considerable time. In both lineages, but particularly in the more 'gracile' one, there is also some evolutionary change, and this has to be taken into account. These East African fossils have helped to fill in the time gap that previously existed between the last undoubted *A. africanus* from Makapansgat and the earliest *H. erectus* from Java–the period between about $1\frac{3}{4}$ million and $\frac{3}{4}$ million years ago. Not surprisingly, the filling of the gap has caused some confusion. The previous absence of fossils from part of the lineage provided a convenient boundary for dividing up the continuum into 'species'.

The earliest of these East African hominid remains, a lower end of a humerus, comes from Kanapoi in north-western Kenya from deposits which are older than a lava flow dated at $2\frac{1}{2}$ million years. They are probably as much as 4 million years old. No stone tools have been recovered from these deposits. Multivariate statistical analysis of the humeral fragment aligns it unquivocally with man rather than with the chimpanzee, the hominoid most similar to man in this anatomical region. Professors Bryan Patterson and F. Clark Howell, the describers of this fragment, believe that it represents *A. africanus* rather than *A. robustus*.

Professor Patterson has also recovered a hominid lower-jaw fragment with one molar intact from Lothagan in Kenya. This fossil may be as much as 5 million years old. Recently Professor Howell has reported a series of hominid teeth from deposits at Omo in Ethiopia. These finds range in age from 2 to 4 million years, and represent at least two species, one of which resembles South African *A. africanus* and the other East African *Homo habilis*, to be discussed later. The Omo site is potentially one of the most valuable in the world for research into human origins, and may well rank in importance with that to which we now turn.

Perhaps the most magnificent site in the world to have yielded hominid fossils is Olduvai Gorge in Tanzania. The sediments were laid down during the Pleistocene in or around a lake. They are of volcanic origin as well as being deposited by the lake, and some of the volcanic material has been dated by the K/A method. Other corroborative means of dating have also been employed, and the base of the sequence is now one of the best dated regions in the world. Recently a river has cut through the sediments to form a gorge in the sides of which successive layers are clearly displayed.

The Drs Leakey have worked in the Gorge on and off since the 1930s, and their magnificent efforts have been amply rewarded. The deposits have been divided by geologists into several beds, the lowest and oldest being Bed I, the next Bed II, and so on. Bed I and the lower part of Bed II are African 'early Pleistocene', upper Villafranchian equivalents. The base of Bed I is 1·9 million years old, and falls almost exactly on the Pliocene-Pleistocene boundary. The upper parts of Bed II, plus Beds III and IV, are middle Pleistocene. No dates are available from Olduvai for this part of the sequence, although dating is possible from another site, Peninj, with a fauna and tool technology similar to upper Bed II. From Peninj it can be estimated that an age of 700,000 years would apply to parts of upper Bed II, so possibly what is called the 'middle Pleistocene' in Africa runs from more than 1 million years ago to less than 500,000 years (an estimate for the age of the top of Bed II). It is quite likely that the middle Pleistocene of Europe, defined on faunal and geological grounds, is not time-synchronous with that in Africa. Only absolute dates from geologically well-known European regions can clear up this problem.

Zinjanthropus

As mentioned above, there are two main hominid lineages represented at Olduvai, and I shall treat these briefly in turn. These lineages consist respectively of 'robust' and 'gracile' hominids and will initially be described as such. In 1959 Dr Mary Leakey found the greater part of the skull of a robust hominid in Bed I. Subsequent dating indicated that the skull is around $1\frac{3}{4}$ million years old. Dr Louis Leakey published a note describing this specimen and listing characters which he believed separated it from both South African hominids. He gave it a new name, *Zinjanthropus boisei*, distinct from *Paranthropus* and *Australopithecus*. Many workers have claimed that *Z. boisei* should have been classified with *Paranthropus*, the general point being that on superficial analysis the Olduvai skull (hominid 5 in the Olduvai numbered sequence) shows the low-

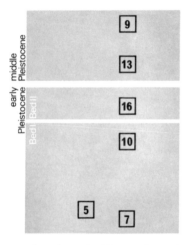

Chronology of Olduvai Beds I and II, showing the ages of some of the main hominid finds. Hominids 7, 10, 16, 13 and 9 are of the Australopithecus and Homo lineages; hominid 5 is Zinjanthropus boisei. Opposite top: part of the Olduvai Gorge in Tanzania, where Mary and Louis Leakey have discovered traces of human occupation dating back to early Pleistocene times. Bottom: site of the excavation of Zinjanthropus at Olduvai

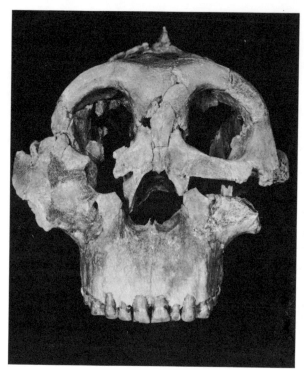

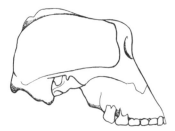

Diagram and photograph of the skull of Olduvai hominid 5, Zinjanthropus. (Tobias prefers to assign the Zinjanthropus skull to Australopithecus; the author to Paranthropus.)

slung braincase, small front teeth and large cheek teeth of *Paranthropus* from Swartkrans. A very detailed study of the skull by Professor Tobias reaches somewhat different conclusions. From a study just of skull and teeth, Tobias concludes that the two South African species and Olduvai hominid 5 should be classified in just one genus—*Australopithecus*. Although *A. boisei* shows resemblances both to *A. africanus* and to *A. robustus*, Tobias believes that *A. boisei* is in the same lineage as *robustus*, though ancestral to it. He mentions the possibility of crossing between the *A. boisei/A. robustus* line and that of *A. africanus*.

Things are greatly complicated here by the distorted nature of *robustus* skull specimens, the probable time difference between Olduvai and Swartkrans, and the considerable geographical distance between them. However, the Olduvai and Swartkrans samples do show a number of similarities in general skull shape, particularly in the rather distinctive low set of the brain-case on the face and in the flattened facial region. They are similar too in that the premolars are molarized, although much more so in Olduvai hominid 5 than in *robustus*. Indeed, the cheek tooth area of the East African form is some 40 per cent greater than the *robustus* average. This may reflect body size difference as we have already noted. Associated with these huge cheek teeth, the Olduvai skull is even more massively constructed and buttressed than those from Swartkrans. The face is also longer, and this means that the (un-known) lower jaw of Olduvai hominid 5 would have had a much higher ascending ramus than any of the Swartkrans mandibles. All these features point to the fact that more grinding was being accomplished in the Olduvai hominid than in *robustus* and the skull was buttressed against greater chewing stresses. The transi-tion from premolars to canines is also more abrupt than in any other hominids, yet one can envisage that a *robustus* with greatly enlarged teeth could easily end up looking like Olduvai hominid 5, or vice versa.

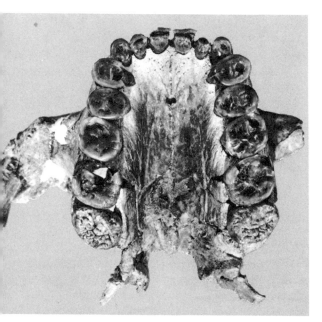

Palate and dentition of Zinjanthro-pus, notable for the great size of the molars and premolars in relation to the canines and incisors

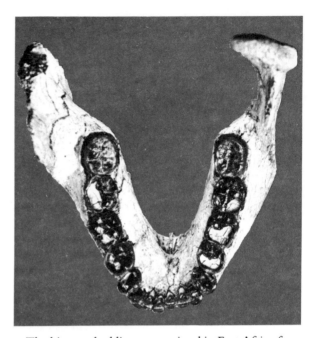

The mandible found in 1964 at Peninj, near Olduvai

The big-toothed lineage persisted in East Africa for a long time. Traces of this form are present at the top of Bed II, 0·5 or 0·6 million years ago, and also at Peninj, close to Olduvai in Tanzania. The Peninj specimen, a mandible, comes from deposits of early middle Pleistocene age, correlative with Olduvai upper Bed II; as I have already mentioned, Peninj can be dated to around 0·7 million years. The mandible shows great molarization of the premolars, in this feature and in overall size being closer to Olduvai hominid 5 than to *robustus*. However, the ascending ramus is lower than is indicated for the Olduvai form and Tobias has assigned this mandible to *robustus*. His idea is that one lineage is represented in East and South Africa, the earlier members of which were large-toothed like Olduvai 5. The lineage evolved by becoming smaller-toothed and shorter faced, and appears as the Swartkrans and Peninj material in early middle and late early Pleistocene time. This is certainly possible, and the reduction in tooth size could be due to crossing with a smaller-toothed lineage like *A. africanus* as Tobias has suggested. But the tiny samples on which this is based are really insufficient for definite schemes of this kind. The East and South African robust forms could equally well represent parallel, closely related lineages which none the less might be treated as separate species. Only by the discovery of further material can we sort this out. Provisionally I shall classify the East African material as *Paranthropus boisei*.

A clavicle and parts of a hand from Olduvai belong perhaps to *A. boisei*. They suggest that in body size the Olduvai form equalled or exceeded *robustus* from Swartkrans. The hand bones are peculiar and come either from an arboreal type or, more likely, from one which was capable of very powerful grasping.

When first found, Olduvai hominid 5 was thought to represent the maker of the Oldowan stone tools, the industry typical of Bed I and lower Bed II at Olduvai. The Oldowan was once thought to be characterized by small chopping 'pebble tools'. But the Drs Leakey have now excavated a number of whole living floors and so have an excellent sample of the tools actually made. Recent reports by Dr Mary Leakey have shown a surprising variety of tool types (surprising, I should add, only because nobody anticipated this much variety!). The individual tool categories show considerable variability in form. Types of tools were not particularly standardized at this stage. Some tools are hardly recognizable as such; others would not be out of place in much later and more defined industries. As tool-making technologies developed, tools were to become more elaborate, more diverse, and also more standardized. Since other sorts of hominids have been found at Olduvai, it is impossible to tie one particular hominid species to tool-making. Perhaps too it is wrong to think of these early tools as comprising one industry. In their early stages, one industry might well look much like another and the Oldowan tradition could be viewed as a technological complex; different early hominids might each be manufacturing very similar-looking tools. Again, this sort of thing is going to be very difficult to prove.

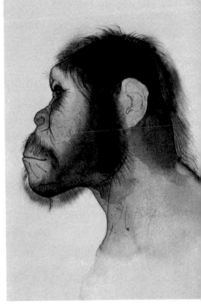

An imaginative reconstruction of the head of Zinjanthropus

A flaked-pebble chopping tool found at Olduvai

The robust lineages, both in East and South Africa, show numerous specializations of skull, jaws, teeth and post-cranial skeleton. They differed morphologically from the sort of hominid we find at Sterkfontein and Makapansgat. What these differences represent in terms of behaviour and ecology cannot be determined. It is probable, however, that these hominids contributed few if any genes to later species and we shall therefore turn to the second Olduvai lineage of more gracile types.

Homo habilis

A juvenile mandible was found in 1961 close to the base of Bed I, a little lower than the site from which Olduvai hominid 5 came. For this reason it received the colloquial name 'pre-Zinj', one which should now be forgotten. In 1964 it was given a proper scientific name, *Homo habilis*, by Leakey, Tobias and Napier. In the original description a variety of material from Beds I and II was included, firmly or tentatively, in *Homo*

The Olduvai hominid-7 mandible, predicated of Homo habilis

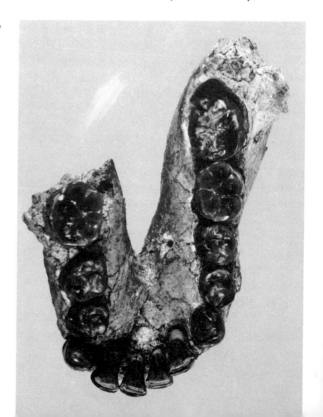

habilis. Tobias has since stated his belief that the Bed I material, containing the type specimen, is *H. habilis,* while the younger material is sufficiently different to be left out of *H. habilis.* The two groups none the less clearly belong to a single lineage.

Considering the Bed I material first, the type mandible (Olduvai hominid 7) contrasts markedly with what we would expect for the lower jaw of *boisei,* and also with those of *robustus.* It is much more similar to *A. africanus,* differing from it in the relative narrowness of the premolars, and in a few other features. On dental grounds alone, *H. habilis* and *A. africanus* could represent either subspecies of one species, or closely related species. In overall tooth area and relative proportions of front and back teeth, the two groups are quite similar. However, the Olduvai teeth show very little crowding, while those in *A. africanus* jaws are frequently compressed together. This may be an important difference, but its significance has not yet been investigated.

From the same individual, Olduvai 7, come parts of the skull—fragments of the parietal bones. These bones have been used to estimate the individual's total skull volume, and the result comes out—naturally approximately, since only the parietal bones are known—to around 640 or 650 c.c., above the average and known range for six *A. africanus* skulls. But just how significant this difference is has been hard to evaluate. There is just one estimate from Bed I Olduvai, four from Sterkfontein, and one each from Taung and Makapansgat. If the somewhat dangerous step of merging the South African skulls into one group is taken, the sample is still only six skulls. Just the same problem applies to the teeth and it is extremely difficult to evaluate the significance of the differences which undoubtedly do exist between South and East African hominids. Bearing this in mind, it is possible to state cautiously once again that on this character of brain size the two samples could just about represent two subspecies, or perhaps more likely closely related species. Remember that these two sets of hominids are spread over something like two thousand miles, and are likely to be of different geological age. At least part of *A. africanus* is probably older than Bed I Olduvai, and so *H. habilis* could represent a more advanced phase of the *A. africanus* lineage. I shall discuss this more fully later on.

Bones from a juvenile hand probably belong to this individual (hominid 7) too. The hand bones were recovered from the same site at Olduvai and belong to at least two individuals. According to Dr Alan Walker it is possible that three are in fact sampled. Two, including the juvenile, seem rather closer to modern man than the third, which has already been discussed as possibly belonging to *A. boisei*. The juvenile bones almost certainly belong to *H. habilis*, along with the matching adult bones. One of the hand bones, the capitate, although badly weathered, resembles a capitate from

The Olduvai hand (Homo habilis)

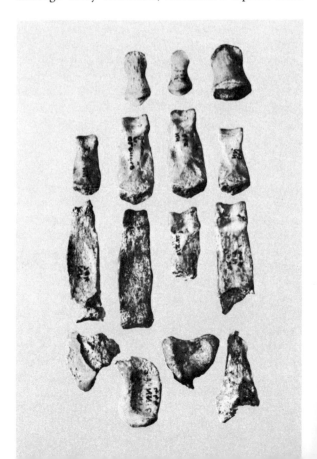

Sterkfontein. All that can be said of the hand is that it does not differ too greatly from that of *H. sapiens*, nor possibly from that of *A. africanus*. In size it is quite close to a moderate-sized modern hand. The clavicle from this site, already discussed with *A. boisei*, is large and robust. It might possibly belong with *H. habilis*, but its size points rather to the more robust hominid.

Another individual, Olduvai hominid 8, comes from the same site as the juvenile *H. habilis* and consists of the adult hand bones mentioned above and a particularly magnificent specimen consisting of the greater part of the left foot. The foot is of small size, but is clearly very similar to that of *H. sapiens*. Functionally, it was adapted to habitual bipedalism. The tarsal bones fit together in such a way as to form longitudinal and transverse arches with ligaments and muscles supporting these arch systems just as in modern man. The big toe was set closely parallel to the others, and the outer side of the foot was relatively robust, indicating that weight transmission ran around the outer border of the foot, across the heads of the metatarsals, and through the great toe–similar to transmission in *H. sapiens*. One or two minor points suggest that the foot was a shade less well adapted to striding than in modern man.

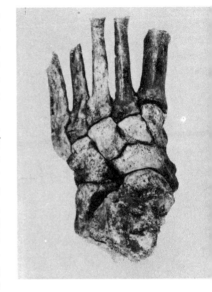

The Olduvai hominid-8 foot bones (Homo habilis)

A few other remains are known from lower Bed I, and probably belong to *H. habilis*. Teeth come from a site low in Bed I, and from the original site of Olduvai hominid 5. Along with the *A. boisei* skull were also found a tibia and fibula. These are small, delicate bones and would fit nicely on to the *H. habilis* foot. They indicate upright posture, almost as refined as in *H. sapiens*, and come from an individual little more than 4 feet tall; they belong more properly with *H. habilis* than with the robust hominid.

Summing up what we know of early Bed I *H. habilis*, the material comes from the early Pleistocene and hence our comparisons should be with *Australopithecus africanus* from the South African early Pleistocene. The East African form is a lightly built, small-brained, bipedal hominid, very similar to *A. africanus* although the latter has a somewhat smaller brain and shows slight differences in the dentition. There are two possible interpretations. As I have said previously, these samples could be subspecies, albeit rather different ones, within the same species, and such differences as do exist could be due to the fact that *H. habilis* is geologically younger and hence more evolved than *A. africanus*. Alternatively, these two samples could belong to two separate but related lineages, roughly equivalent perhaps to two similar but geographically separated baboon species. If they belong to different lineages – to different species – we are faced with the problem of how to classify the Olduvai material; as *Homo habilis* or *Australopithecus habilis*? Of course, *H. habilis* and *A. africanus* do not differ as much as two living genera; this is hardly to be expected since they apparently evolved only recently from a common ancestor. Yet if it can be shown that *H. habilis* is ancestral to later hominids, while *A. africanus* is not, then with some justice *habilis* could be assigned to *Homo*. Also if *H. habilis* is *the* tool-maker at Olduvai, and none of the other early hominids fabricated tools, then many anthropologists would choose to include the East African form in *Homo*. It has become almost a matter of dogma that the manufacture of tools of a set and regular pattern is necessary and sufficient cause for classifying a hominid in *Homo*.

For the moment, however, I prefer to believe that *habilis*, although a tool-maker, was not *the* tool-maker and that evidence for the tool-making abilities of *A. africanus* may be forthcoming. So, provisionally, I should like to group *africanus* and *habilis* in the same genus, *Australopithecus*. I think it possible that they are members of a single species, which would therefore be called *Australopithecus africanus*, and which would have two subspecies: *A. a. africanus* in South Africa and *A. a. habilis* in East Africa. For the moment I am going to call the Tanzanian material *A. a. habilis*. My reasons for not including this species in *Homo* are given later.

Reviewing the known structure and behaviour of this hominid, what do we have? Creatures no more than 4 feet 6 inches tall, weighing little more than 60 or 70 pounds, showing little or no sexual dimorphism in body size nor in canine size. Indeed the dentition as a whole, and many features of the skull, is typically hominid. The brain was small, between 400 and 700 c.c. but exceeded that of apes of roughly equivalent or greater body size. Yet, although the brain was so small, less than half that of modern man, behaviour was obviously not pongid. The creatures were bipedal and ran and walked much as we do, probably for much the same reasons as living hunter-gatherers do. Evidence drawn particularly from the complete living floors at Olduvai shows that these small creatures were quite successful hunters, killing a variety of large as well as small game. They used their hands and arms as we do for clubbing and throwing, and for making a wide range of tools (at least at Olduvai), for cutting up game after it had been killed, for making other tools and weapons, for preparing skins, for digging up roots, and so on. One particular area at Olduvai preserved evidence for some sort of living structure – a wind-break perhaps – used by the early hominids. By comparing tools and debris on the ancient living floors with materials left behind by living hunter-gatherers it can be deduced that bands were probably composed of about a dozen individuals (perhaps occasionally joining with others to hunt really big game). Bands probably stayed together for several days in one place. No doubt there was division of labour between the sexes, the males hunting while the females foraged for vegetable food and small game; probably females provided most of the food, the males the planning and protection. This type of band structure requires cooperative behaviour of the highest degree between individuals, and little or no 'dominance' as known in non-human primates. This is where the lack of body-size and canine-size dimorphism is so important in providing additional evidence to show that these early forms really were behaving like hominids, and not like apes. Yet, although all this was possible with a small brain, these early hominids would still not have been as intelligent as later ones, however 'intelligence' is defined. Richness and complexity of behaviour, particularly language, may well have been poor.

We should again consider the question of tooth size. Cheek teeth–the chewing teeth–are large in early Pleistocene hominids, particularly when body size is taken into account. Compared to a small chimpanzee with body weight greater than *A. africanus*, the hominid has much the larger teeth. Obviously diets must have been different, and the hominids can hardly have been fruit-eaters like chimps. Exactly what they did eat is hard to tell but perhaps they were adapted for chewing bones as well as meat and vegetable material. The matter is puzzling, and needs further work.

Other East African material

There are good samples of middle Pleistocene hominids from various parts of the world, and although a few of these (or many of them, according to taste) may not be ancestral to later men they are none the less well known. They come from a fairly restricted time period, are best known from Asia, and are much the same in morphology; they have been classified as *H. erectus*. Before Olduvai yielded such an exceptional bounty, early Pleistocene hominids were represented by the 'australopithecines'. The earlier, less specialized hominid, *A. africanus*, was thought of as a good morphological precursor for *H. erectus*. Until the Olduvai discoveries, *A. africanus* was known only from South Africa, and *H. erectus* was best preserved in Asia. So the tentative ancestral-descendant relationship inferred for them should have been qualified in the following way (although it rarely was!). *Australopithecines* did not rapidly migrate to Asia, evolving all the way, to arrive there in the middle Pleistocene as *H. erectus*! Rather, *A. africanus* represented the South African part of an early Pleistocene species which was in fact much more widely distributed. The same caution applies to *H. erectus* and the middle Pleistocene; known specimens inevitably sample only poorly the actual species distribution. These samples–one African, the other Asian

–could quite easily have belonged to the same lineage, which would have been at all times much more widely distributed than just the known, sampled, areas.

It is the parts of this lineage between early and middle Pleistocene which are now being filled in. Because this evolving line was a whole complex of inter-meshing subspecific populations, waxing and waning and merging through time, the 'intermediate' fossils often do not come up to expectations and for this reason have caused difficulties. Of course these fossils are 'intermediate' only in the sense that they fall in time and space between two previously known clusters of fossils. These samples, and the gap between them, had been used to split the evolving lineage up into 'species' but the boundaries between them are obviously arbitrary and will automatically become blurred and disappear as more fossils are found to fill in the remaining gaps.

The early Bed I material at Olduvai has caused enough confusion and argument as it is. Having chosen between our alternatives, and decided, provisionally, that *A. africanus* and some of the Olduvai material belong to one lineage and can probably best be grouped in one species, by thus expanding the earlier concept of *A. africanus* we have gone a long way towards closing the gap between *H. erectus* and its antecedent.

From Olduvai too have come fossils which fill the time gap between these earlier hominids and *H. erectus*. Towards the top of Bed I there is hominid 10, consisting merely of the last element of the big toe of a hominid. It might strike you that this is not a particularly promising piece to use as evidence, but in fact it is. Detailed multivariate statistical analysis has shown that it is clearly hominid, a hominid in which weight transmission during striding and other aspects of gait were exactly as in *H. sapiens*. This fossil probably belongs to the same lineage as the earlier Bed I fossils.

Two further hominids are of interest here. They are from Bed II and were described originally as *Homo habilis*, but later moved by Tobias into a category of 'suspended judgement'. The first (hominid 16) is known by a skull from a site in Bed II below the faunal break representing the boundary between early and middle Pleistocene. The age is probably around $1\frac{1}{4}$ million years, perhaps more. The skull has been badly trampled by cattle but after several attempts Professor Tobias has produced a very plausible reconstruction. Tobias believes that the skull is not in the same lineage as the Bed I hominids but represents instead 'an australopithecine'. Presumably he regards it as closer to *A. africanus* than to *A. robustus*. However, the dentition also resembles *H. erectus*, and the skull as last reconstructed could well fit in as an intermediate between early Pleistocene forms and middle Pleistocene ones. The cranial capacity is 640 c.c., the skull thin-walled and rather more rounded and less elongated than in *H. erectus*. At present, I prefer to keep the stage as uncluttered as possible and to place hominid 16 in the main lineage leading to later hominids.

The second hominid (hominid 13) is known by skull pieces from a site in Bed II just above the faunal break, that is, in the middle Pleistocene as it is defined in this area. Absolute age although difficult to assess would be perhaps 1 million years. The skull is small, delicate, and gracefully rounded with a volume of some 620 c.c., and it is quite similar to *A. africanus* from South Africa. It also resembles closely the known parts of hominid 7, and with little doubt belongs to the same lineage. Associated with this skull are parts of upper and lower

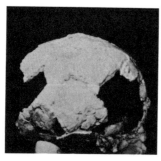

The Olduvai hominid-13 skull bones

jaws and teeth. These again resemble hominid 7, although they are somewhat smaller. The teeth of hominid 13 have been compared by Professors Tobias and von Koenigswald with those of the earliest known *Homo erectus* from Java (to be discussed later). They are indeed closely similar and represent to Tobias and von Koenigswald the same 'grade' of evolution, which presumably means that they are rather similar. These similarities have caused Tobias to remove hominid 13 from his concept of *H. habilis*, and to regard it as an unnamed *Homo* species; others have jumped the gun and transferred it to *H. erectus*. However, the skull of the Javanese *H. erectus* is known, and it differs markedly from hominid 13. It has a larger volume (750 c.c.), is longer and lower, and has much thicker bony walls. The fact that jaws and teeth are similar in the two forms should not detract from the fact that the skulls do contrast markedly, more so than hominid 13 and South African *A. africanus*. (Interestingly, hominid 16 would make a passable intermediate between the two.)

If hominid 13 does belong to *H. erectus* we shall need to alter greatly our ideas about the morphological limits of this species. Of course this is a perfectly justifiable procedure. But the problem only rises because this specimen is a temporal and morphological intermediate between two time-successive species, previously divided quite arbitrarily because of gaps in knowledge. This is a fossil with jaws and teeth rather like *H. erectus* and a skull rather like *A. africanus*. It can be assigned to either species, but in doing so the morphological limits of one have to be altered. An intermediate species could be created but this does not solve our difficulties, for at this level the name given to a fossil is relatively unimportant once we know which lineage it belongs to and its temporal position. More interesting and important are the trends, morphological and behavioural, which can be inferred from the fossils.

The example of hominid 13 shows how dangerous it is to call *'Telanthropus'* from Swartkrans a *H. erectus* just because of the small jaws and teeth. The age of those deposits makes it much more likely that in skull structure the Swartkrans hominid resembled hominid 13 from Olduvai, and in this sense is closer to *A. africanus* from Sterkfontein (as we have already concluded).

Tool-making appears abruptly in Africa at the beginning of the Pleistocene. Quite likely, tool-making once invented rapidly became widespread; possibly tool types were quite diversified from the start. Earlier ideas suggested that the origins of stone tool-making were long drawn out, and that tool diversity developed only gradually. Dr Glynn Isaac has recently pointed out that this now seems improbable, at least as far as formal tool-making traditions are concerned. (That is, ruling out tool use in Pliocene and Miocene time.) This sudden invention, and rapid spread, of tool-making may well imply that there was little or no difference in 'brain-power', behavioural potential, or however it is described, before and after its invention—a most important point.

Reviewing the evidence, we have at least two lineages of early Pleistocene and late Pliocene hominids, one group of which was robust and big-toothed. These forms may have been tool-makers. They appear to have become extinct early in the middle Pleistocene. The other smaller-bodied line invented tool-making in the latest Pliocene and probably had evolved by the middle Pleistocene into *H. erectus*. During this long time period, covering at least 1 million years, tool-making changed very little (again contrary to old ideas of steady change towards the hand-axe industries). There is little evidence for the introduction of new tools or for much refinement in the old ones during this period. Nor do the hominids appear to change much. Perhaps brain size increased a little, and tooth size might have gone down, but as yet we do not have sufficient, well-dated samples to test this. The archaeological evidence indicates that hominids were widespread in Africa (generally outside the central forest area) during the early Pleistocene. They were probably in Europe too at this time, and perhaps in Asia as well.

The lineages of early Pleistocene hominids may have hybridized, may have exchanged genetic 'information', yet none of them seems materially to have affected the course of evolution of any other. This is the type of crossing that can be seen between living species rather than subspecies; I think it quite justified to treat these separate lineages as distinct species. Following this long period of quiescence a new type of hominid evolved in the middle Pleistocene. The morphological differences which exist, on average, between the early and middle Pleistocene forms are sufficient, I believe, to justify their placement in separate genera, *Australopithecus* and *Homo*. Now let us turn our attention to these later hominids.

Middle Pleistocene hominids are quite widely distributed throughout the Old World, and are found in Asia as well as Africa. The tools made by middle Pleistocene men broadly resemble those of the early Pleistocene although tool types became more refined and more standardized. In Africa, Europe and western Asia a new type of tool, the hand-axe, appears during this time to join the array of 'pebble-tools'. The appearance of this tool–probably not actually an axe but a digging or scraping tool–may have been due to the invention in certain areas of a particular technique, the ability (according to Glynn Isaac) to strike flakes greater than ten centimeters in length as the raw blanks of future hand-axes. So the presence or absence of hand-axes need not imply anything particularly profound about behavioural changes.

The first middle Pleistocene hominids were recovered by Eugene Dubois in eastern central Java in the late nineteenth century. He named his material *Pithecanthropus erectus* in 1891. Subsequently these hominids have been transferred to our own genus to become *Homo erectus*, although they are still occasionally called 'pithecanthropines', an unfortunate colloquial term. The fact that this species was first recovered from Asian deposits, and only later from Africa, should not lead to the belief that it was an Asian species which spread to Africa!

Early Palaeolithic flint hand-axe from the Thames Valley, probably less an axe than a digging and scraping tool

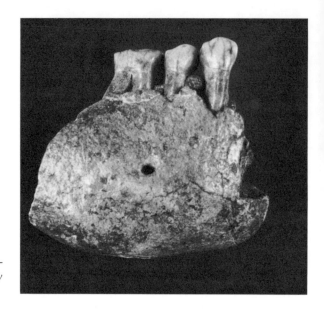

The Meganthropus mandibular fragment found in Java in 1939 by G.H.R. von Koenigswald

Java man

The Javanese so-called middle Pleistocene sequence consists of two sets of deposits containing similar but distinct faunas. The earlier fauna found in beds on various parts of the island is termed the Djetis; the later, the Trinil. Attempts have been made to correlate these in European terms, but such efforts have been to little avail, since the European earlier middle Pleistocene is so poorly understood. Absolute dates from Java are fairly good; there is a K/A date of 0·5 million years from close to the top of Trinil age beds, and a date of 0·7 million years for the bottom. The Djetis age beds are probably approaching 1 million years old. In terms of the important East African sequence, the Djetis and Trinil faunas cover approximately the upper parts of Bed II at Olduvai; that is, they may well run back to the end of the early Pleistocene as defined in East Africa.

Rather than discussing finds in the order of their discovery, I prefer to list them stratigraphically from oldest to youngest. A mandible fragment found before the last war by Professor von Koenigswald comes from beds of Djetis age. It was described originally as

Meganthropus palaeojavanicus because of its massive construction and great size. It has been interpreted variously as a *Paranthropus robustus* (by Robinson), as a large *Homo erectus* (by Le Gros Clark), and it has been compared with Olduvai Bed I hominid 7 (by Tobias and von Koenigswald). These disagreements actually underline the very great dental and mandibular similarities between all these groups. The find could be similar to the Olduvai specimens and still represent a somewhat earlier stage than the first (Trinil) *Homo erectus*. I prefer to classify it with *Homo erectus* for the moment, at least until the skull is known. The skulls which are known from the Djetis levels are clearly *Homo erectus*. A small skull from an individual of less than 5 or 6 years (perhaps as young as 2 or 3 years) already shows the beginnings of brow ridges, marked post-orbital constrictions, and a projecting occipital region. As an adult, its brain volume could hardly have exceeded 800 c.c.

Parts of an adult skull are also known from this level. The back of a skull plus parts of the face and most of

The Modjokerto infant skull (Homo erectus), found in Java in 1936 in a bed of Pleistocene sands and marine sediments

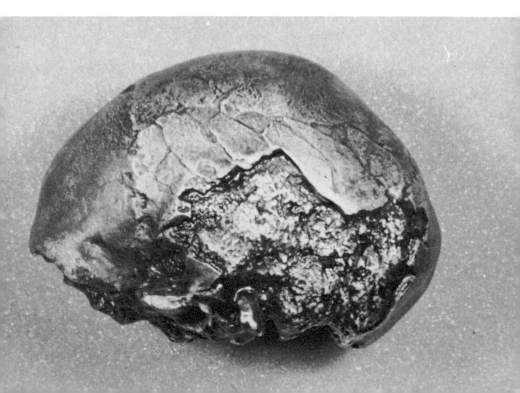

the upper teeth have been restored by von Koenigswald using other Javanese material to produce a very
reasonable reconstruction. A mandible, although not
associated with the skull, comes from the same deposits
and is similar enough to be considered as part of the
same individual. This composite specimen is the one
compared by Tobias and von Koenigswald with
hominid 13 from Olduvai. The dentitions are very
similar as I have already described, and the gap between
them is nicely filled by hominid 16 from Olduvai. The
Javanese skull, however, is long and low with large
brow ridges. The bones of the braincase are very thick
indeed, much thicker than in the earlier East and South
African hominids. There are quite marked contrasts in
shape between hominid 13 and the *Homo erectus* skull.
The skull volumes are a little different, 620 c.c. for the
Olduvai form and 750 c.c. for the Javanese. The
Olduvai hominid 16 skull is of 640 c.c. and in shape
again fills the gap between the two, although like
hominid 13 it is still thin-walled. The principal differences between these *A. africanus* (? *A. habilis*) and
H. erectus are due to the fact that the *H. erectus* skull is
longer and hence (because the brain is still small) lower.
It is broader too and so is the palate. Because the skull is
long and low the forehead is flatter, the brow ridges
more pronounced, and the occipital angulated instead
of evenly rounded. All these features may be due to the
fact that the *H. erectus* brains grew with the bigger
stature of the Javanese men, producing a clear change
in skull shape as the relative proportions of the cranium
changed. Increases in size generally involve changes in
shape and this must not be forgotten (note for example
the contrasts between the shape of male and female
baboon skulls). Although the exact stature of the
earliest Javanese hominids is unknown, they were
probably taller than *A. africanus*. So the Olduvai skulls
could theoretically represent a state ancestral to *Homo
erectus* before these increases in body size. The transition
between the stages was nevertheless complex.

The first finds of *Homo erectus* made by Dubois came
from the Trinil zone and consisted of a skull cap and a

femur. The skull cap is primitive in morphology and barely larger than those from Djetis beds. When first found, it was considered to be an excellent missing link between men and apes. Now, of course, it is known that this individual is millions of years separated from its ape ancestors, and that it really is pointless to talk in those terms. The femur resembles closely that of a modern man of average height. The femur came from an individual 5 foot 7 inches at least, and one perfectly adapted to upright walking. At first there was some argument as to whether this femur represented *Homo sapiens* living alongside *Homo erectus*, or perhaps came from later beds. As with the South African early hominids, there was a great reluctance to associate man-like limbs with primitive skulls. However, chemical tests have shown that the femur and the skull are contemporaneous, and five more femora were found in Dubois' collections showing that the original was no aberration. Without doubt skulls and limbs are associated. Several other skulls from the Trinil levels confirm the general morphology—long, low skulls

The skull cap found by Eugene Dubois at Trinil, Java, in 1891

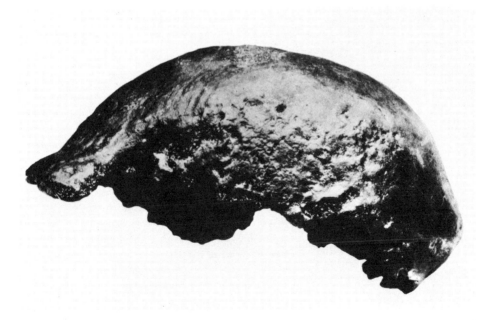

with big brow ridges and projecting occipital regions. The Trinil skulls vary in volume from 775 to 975 c.c., and appear to be a little larger on average than those from the Djetis. I have already mentioned changes in skull shape from the *A. africanus* stage. Since the brain does not overgrow the orbits–because the whole face is large and projecting–the frontal bone is very flat, and large brow ridges surmount the eyes.

The increase in body size over early Pleistocene hominids is quite marked; from something around 4 feet to 4 feet 6 inches, to an average of more than 5 feet 6 inches (at least for males). As I mentioned, this may account for at least some of the increase in brain size.

All these Javanese specimens are more than 0·5 million years old and may be older than 0·6 or 0·7 million years. A fossil skull and jaw are known from about the same time level in northwest China, from Lantien. The deposits are said to be equivalent to the Djetis levels. The skull is small and primitive like *Homo erectus* from Java; the cranial capacity is only 780 c.c. The mandible is interesting in that there is no evidence at all of the third molar, the first recorded case of a condition which is becoming increasingly frequent in *Homo sapiens*.

Pekin man

Much more complete and better known fossils come from northeast China, near Pekin, at Choukoutien. From 1921 onwards a large number of fossil skulls were recovered there. These were lost during the war– a terrible tragedy–although fortunately good casts still exist. Remains were recovered of some 16 skulls in varying states of preservation, a dozen or so mandibles, many teeth, and some limb bones. Originally these specimens were described as *Sinanthropus pekinensis*. Later it was realized that they represented a subspecies of the same species as the Javanese forms and so were reclassified as *Pithecanthropus pekinensis*. Finally, when the name *Pithecanthropus* was dispensed with, they became *Homo erectus pekinensis*.

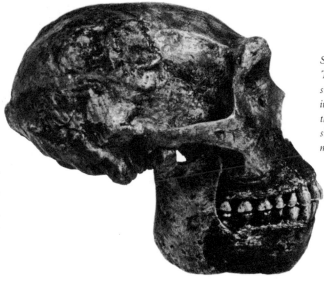

Skull of Java man (Homo erectus). This reconstruction by von Koenig-swald is based on fossil remains found in the Djetis strata at Sangiran in the 1930s. In most respects except size the teeth resemble those of modern man

The skulls have large projecting faces and moderate brow ridges. They are long and still rather low, although not so low as the Lantian or Java skulls. The occiput is less sharply angled too. Altogether the skulls are filled out more, because the brain volume was larger than in the skulls we previously discussed. Seven tolerably complete skulls show that the volume ranged from at least 850 to 1300 c.c., and one would expect larger samples to show a larger range. The average is around 1050 c.c. The skeletal material is not particularly extensive but what is known does not differ significantly from modern man. Individuals may have been somewhat smaller than the Javanese forms.

Dating Choukoutien is a little difficult. No rocks suitable for absolute dating are known, but if long range correlations are tentatively accepted, the deposits appear to fit into the European sequence at approximately the beginning of the Mindel glaciation. Dating this in a European context is difficult, but an age of at least 0·4 to 0·5 million years would not be far off the mark.

A great deal of evidence from Choukoutien shows that *Homo erectus* ate vegetable as well as animal food

Skull of Pekin man (also Homo erectus), as restored by P. Weiden-reich. This is an adult female example

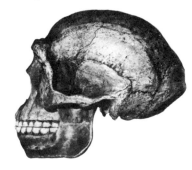

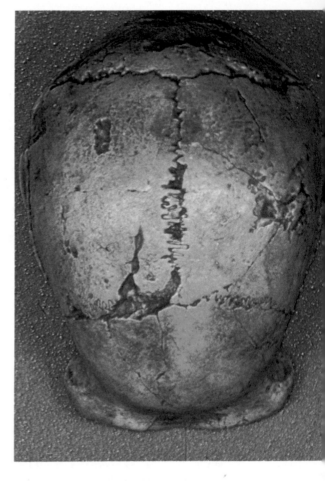

Right: skull cap of Pekin man. Opposite top: excavation in progress near Choukoutien, China, at the site of the discovery of Pekin man. Bottom: an imaginative reconstruction of the life of Pekin man

and was a very successful big-game hunter. From Choukoutien too come signs of the first use of fire, used no doubt both for cooking food and for warming bodies. Dr Edmund Leach has this to say about cooking:

> It isn't a biological necessity that you should cook food, it is a custom, a symbolic act, a piece of magic which transforms the substance and removes the contamination of 'otherness'. Raw food is dirty and dangerous; cooked food is clean and safe. So already, even at the very beginning, man somehow saw himself as 'other' than nature. The cooking of food

Maurice Wilson 1950

is both an assertion of this otherness and a means of getting rid of the anxiety which otherness generates.

The *Homo erectus* specimens from Asia cover a fair period of time, from about 1 million years for the Lantien and Djetis level specimens, through 0·7 million for the Trinil, to about 0·5 million for Choukoutien. There appears to have been some evolution during this time, particularly in brain size, the average of which creeps up steadily from 700 or 800 c.c. to over 1000 c.c. These eastern forms are associated with pebble-type tools; hand-axes do not appear in this area or do so only sporadically. The Asian *Homo erectus* fossils are sampled from two closely related subspecies.

At approximately the same time in Africa, similar types of men were living. From Ternifine in Algeria have come three mandibles which resemble those from Choukoutien. A parietal bone is similar too, down to the markings left on the internal side by the arteries supplying the blood to the outside of the brain. These finds are associated with early hand-axes and a fauna like that of upper Bed II at Olduvai. A cranium of *Homo erectus* (hominid 9) has been found at Olduvai in upper Bed II. The cranial volume is 1000 c.c., like that at Choukoutien. The skull is long and low, with a projecting occipital. Although basically similar to the Asian *Homo erectus*, the African forms do show a few differences. For example, the Olduvai skull has enormous, thick projecting brow ridges, bigger than can

Ternifine I, one of three mandibles found at Ternifine, Algeria, in 1954. Of an adult, probably male, it is nevertheless remarkable for its size and robustness, and bears a strong resemblance to mandibles found at Choukoutien

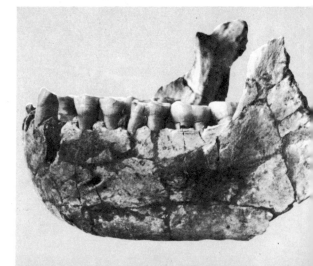

be found in men from Choukoutien, and much more similar to some later African hominids.

This emphasizes two points. At this particular time all populations however widely distributed seem to be quite closely connected genetically; they apparently represent subspecies within a single species. But populations also show continuity and connections through time with other populations. Earlier African populations are therefore likely to contribute more genes to later ones than are earlier, or later, Asian populations. Therefore, earlier Africans are likely to resemble later African ones more closely than are early Asians. At any one time level, all hominids within a species are more or less similar to each other, yet there are also lineal similarities within a particular area (as we have already seen at Olduvai, and also in Java). Carleton Coon has called these 'grade' and 'line' similarities respectively.

In the earlier part of the middle Pleistocene, up to about 0·5 million years ago, primitive members of *Homo* are found in Africa and Asia. They might well have originated in either continent. It would probably be a mistake to think of their origin as occurring in a

Olduvai hominid 9 skull fragment. Despite the very prominent brow ridges, it, also, is basically similar to Asian examples of Homo erectus

small restricted area; it would have been considerably more widespread.

What about this origin, presumably from early Pleistocene *A. africanus* stock of South, East and North African deposits? Dr Leakey believes that the early hominids at Olduvai have nothing at all to do with *H. erectus*, but rather evolved directly into *H. sapiens*, presumably in East Africa. I think it would be a mistake to envisage such highly localized evolution. Unfortunately, we do not have sufficient samples from the various subspecies which must have existed during early and middle Pleistocene time. If we did have more material we could sort out our grade and line relationships, unravel evolution within subspecific lineages, and tie these lineages into the fabric of one species.

Choosing for the moment the simpler hypothesis, let us assume that most early Pleistocene forms had delicate, rounded skulls, large dentitions, and a stature of no more than 4 feet 6 inches or so. Let us also assume that the middle Pleistocene hominids were in general a foot taller; with larger brains; thicker, longer, lower, skulls; and somewhat smaller dentitions. The transition between these two average, or 'polar' types could be tied in with a general increase in body size, for what reason is not known. (There does seem to be a general increase in size of other mammals at this time.) It is obviously necessary to draw a 'species' boundary between the two segments of this single but complex bundle of subspecific lineages. If problems in naming are to be avoided the boundary has to be a 'horizontal'-time boundary. Inevitably, though, the latest *A. africanus* will resemble the earliest *H. erectus* more than either will resemble the 'average' of either 'species' (if indeed these two groups form an ancestor-descendant series).

The trends within this lineage are interesting. There is the increase in body size and the final adjustments in locomotor behaviour. These changes would have increased greatly the potential mobility of individuals and bands, expanding the area they covered, and extending the range of game they could hunt. The first increases in brain size in *H. erectus* could be correlated with these body-size changes, but later there is clearly change in relative size too, probably due to increased size and complexity of nerve cells as well as to increases in their numbers. Teeth and faces seem to shrink a little during this time. Behavioural changes are also apparent. At least some *H. erectus* populations invented hand-axes, and tools were becoming in general more refined and more standardized. Presumably, social and individual behaviour was developing too; perhaps speech was becoming more important. The invention of fire-use, although useful for providing warmth and protection, indicates too that great conceptual and communicative strides had been made in the recognition for men that man was different and apart from other animals. Some would argue that this would only be possible after the appearance of language.

During the remainder of the Pleistocene hominids ever more similar to ourselves emerge. Modern features seem to appear at different rates at different times in different places. The most general trend is one of increasing brain size, from the later *H. erectus* average of about 1000 c.c. to the modern average of 1300 to 1400 c.c. The jaws and teeth, in general, get smaller still. Now there are two ways of coping with an enlarging brain. You can dispose of it as a long, low, broad package, in which case the surrounding skull will also be long, with brow ridges, sloping frontal and projecting occipital region. Alternatively, the same volume can be squeezed into a higher, shorter, narrower space. In this case the brain comes to overlay the orbits and the skull is shaped then like that of modern man, with vaulted frontals showing small or almost non-existent brow ridges and an evenly curved occipital. Along with this shape goes a chin on the lower jaw, to buttress the tooth row during chewing. These two alternatives represent on the one hand earlier and more primitive subspecies of *H. sapiens*, and on the other, later modern types (known now as *H. sapiens sapiens*).

Carleton Coon claims to be able to recognize the crossing of the *erectus/sapiens* 'boundary' (which is of

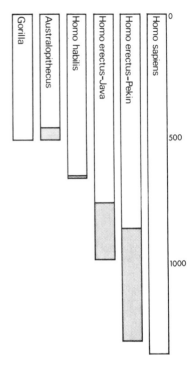

Mean brain volumes (measured in c.c.) of the gorilla and modern man compared with estimated brain volumes of some fossil hominids

course entirely arbitrary) by noting certain cranial features; namely, brain size, the shape and relative proportions of various skull bones, and so on. All these features are, of course, variable within as well as between populations. Theoretically one could find 'erectus' skulls as defined in this sense alongside 'sapiens' skulls, although they would belong to one and the same population. Therefore they could only have one name. If hominids during the middle and later parts of the Pleistocene formed a single species, only one name can be used for any one time. If you start with erectus and wish to end with sapiens, the transition zone has to have a line drawn through it somewhere. I shall discuss the 'somewhere' later on. First, however, I want to discuss later Pleistocene hominids in various parts of the Old World.

Solo man

An excellent sample of fossil men has been recovered from the Solo River in Java. The beds have a late Pleistocene fauna known as the Ngandong, the absolute age of which is unknown. A fair estimate would place it within the last 250,000 years, possibly around 150,000 years ago, although even this is a guess. The hominid population represented is advanced compared

Solo skull (number 6), among Neanderthaloid remains found at Ngandong, central Java, 1931–3

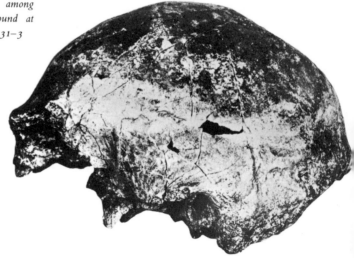

to the earlier *H. erectus* from Java, although its general aspect is primitive. Eleven skulls and two bits of limb bone are known in all. The average brain volume is a little over 1000 c.c. and the face, brow ridges, and occipital region are all still prominent. The Solo population has been described as 'tropical Neanderthalers', but this is rather like calling living Javanese 'tropical Europeans'! What is really meant is that they have big faces, brow ridges, and so on. The word 'Neanderthaler' is being used here in a descriptive sense. I prefer to use the adjective 'neanderthaloid' to refer to those later Pleistocene post-*erectus* populations that show the characters listed above, other than the Neanderthals proper. These Javanese fossil men were sampled from a population which is broadly contemporary with other similar men from different subspecies in adjacent parts of Asia, Europe and Africa.

Modern-looking *H. s. sapiens* may have appeared in this area as long ago as 40,000 years, at Niah in Borneo; the date, based on a C 14 determination, could be wrong, however. The Niah skull is thought to be from a population related in some way to the now-extinct Tasmanians. It seems rather unlikely that Solo population evolved into Niah types But Professor MacIntosh of Sydney University who has done much valuable modern work on early Aboriginal skeletons from Australia believes that he can show some continuity from Solo types through to the living Aboriginals. Speculating from quite inadequate data, this looks rather as though we have a combination of local evolution from *erectus* to modern *sapiens*, through a neanderthaloid phase, coupled with migration of modern *sapiens* into the area, and a subsequent fusion with the more archaic indigenous types. Clearly, in this case the modern and archaic populations would have to be classified in the same species, *Homo sapiens sapiens* (modern) and *H. s. soloensis* (archaic). Whence came the migrants is unknown.

In China a continuous sequence from *erectus* to *sapiens* can be traced, but alternatively it could be argued that successively younger and more advanced specimens represent migrants from some other area. The samples are simply too small.

We are better off, however, in North Africa where there is continuity between *H. erectus* and neanderthaloid populations of *H. sapiens*. The material is practically confined to jaws and teeth and the main trends in these portions of the skeleton are towards smaller size and involve subtle changes in morphology.

Rhodesia man

South of the Sahara is also a story of continuity through to late Pleistocene time. One population in the southern half of Africa is represented by several skulls; from Saldanha in South Africa and Broken Hill in Zambia (some 40,000 to 50,000 years old), as well as other fragmentary remains. Like the Solo group this sample can be described as neanderthaloid. They have brain volumes well within the modern range (1250 to 1300 c.c. for the fossils), yet the skulls are long, faces are large with inflated nasal regions, and brow ridges are

Below and opposite: views of the Neanderthaloid skull of Rhodesian man, found at Broken Hill, Zambia (then Northern Rhodesia), 1921. The brow ridges are more massive than in any other known human skull

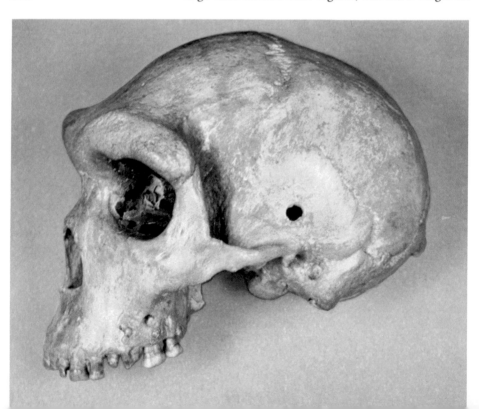

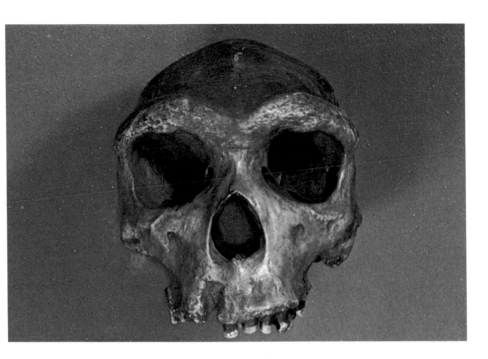

exceptionally thick and projecting. The similarity between the Olduvai Bed II *H. erectus* (hominid 9) and the Broken Hill skull is very obtrusive, and they are almost certainly sampled from a single subspecific lineage which must have evolved slowly in Southern Africa for half a million years or more. The fate of these neanderthaloids (called *H. sapiens rhodesiensis* from the original species name of Broken Hill man) is uncertain. Some workers believe they became extinct without issue; Professor Tobias believes that they may have evolved into Bushmen; while Carleton Coon prefers to connect them with the Negroes. Dr Don Brothwell thinks of them as a line which became extinct, but not without some hybridizing with intrusive modern populations. This last alternative is perhaps closest to the truth, and resembles the most probable sequence of events in southeast Asia. But we still have to explain the evolution of the invading modern populations, for as Professor Tobias has said of earlier attempts to unravel African evolution, 'It was enough to remove the birth of a race to far-off places – and then it became the responsibility of the unfortunate colleagues in those places to worry about how the race had in fact come into being!' The African evidence does point quite clearly to at least some local evolution, and also to mixing on the sort of scale which implies that subspecies rather than species were involved.

There is also some very tantalizing evidence of modern-looking men from Kanjera in Kenya. Fragments of at least three individuals, perhaps more, were found there by Dr Leakey in 1932. A few pieces were *in situ* but most were on the surface. The age of these finds has been debated vigorously; but if we ignore the many 'ifs' involved, it can be put back to at least 60,000 years ago. Professor Tobias has recently re-examined these specimens and finds them fully modern. They have delicate facial regions and vaulted frontals with no brow ridges. The skulls are longish and lowish, but modern in outline. What can be said about these finds? If only the function of brow ridges and big faces were fully understood it would be possible to say something; but until their reduction can be explained, as well as the apparently associated changes in the braincase, we can only grope in the dark. Are these modern-looking skulls genetically related to much later ones? Or do we have (as seems unlikely) parallel evolution? What relationship does the Kanjera sample have to the archaic *H. s. rhodesiensis*? Was there a great deal of variability in skull form during the latter Pleistocene of Africa, so that the average morphology of certain populations gradually shifted through time from archaic to modern? Until there are better samples we shall not even know how typical these skulls are of the population from which they came.

The Heidelberg mandible, found in the Rösch sandpit, near Mauer, 1907

Neanderthal man in Europe

At this juncture we might shift our attention to Europe for a brief discussion of the Neanderthal problem – brief because Europe is a relatively small part of the total area in which hominids were living and should therefore not be given undue importance. It is quite possible that the earliest occupancy of Europe was during the Villafranchian, but fossil men are not known before the middle Pleistocene. The earliest human fossil from Europe is the lower jaw from Mauer, near Heidelberg, in Germany, recovered in 1907. The age is either inter-Mindel or just pre-Mindel and the absolute date is probably over 400,000 years. The jaw shows some similarities to Asian *H. erectus* and some to later European hominids, both to be expected.

Of rather more interest is a sealed inter-Mindel site at Vertesszöllös in Hungary. The site contains evidence of hominid living-floors, hearths and Oldowan-type tools. The age is around 400,000 years. The hominid fossils include a hominid occipital bone, and a handful of teeth. The teeth show many resemblances to Asian *H. erectus*, while the skull looks more advanced. It comes from a large skull, one with a volume of over 1400 c.c., and is more evenly rounded than *H. erectus* skulls. In this respect it approaches *H. sapiens*. The collection of fossils emphasizes the general similarity of all middle Pleistocene men, but also their variability. In Europe 400,000 years ago, some populations already contained individuals which had big brains and rounded occipitals. These Hungarian specimens are close to any boundary between *erectus* and *sapiens* that could be drawn. The boundary will come therefore around 400,000 years ago. Which side of the boundary they fall does not really matter.

The next hominids from Europe are squarely *H. sapiens*. They come from the Mindel-Riss (or Elster-Saäle) interglacial, and, in all probability, date from about 200,000 years ago. Skulls from Steinheim in Germany and Swanscombe in England are closely similar. They had moderate brain volumes (1200 c.c. or so); skulls were long and low with rounded occipitals. Although claims have been made that they are wholly modern-looking, multivariate analysis has shown that they are relatively primitive and not unlike some later Neanderthalers. The face is known only for the Steinheim skull and is moderately large with quite

A vertical view of the Swanscombe skull. The first parietal and an occipital were found in the Barnfield gravel pit, at Swanscombe, Kent, in 1936 and 1937; the second parietal was found as recently as 1955

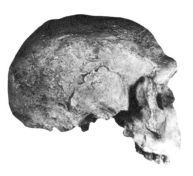

A cast of the Steinheim skull. The original was discovered in the Sigrist gravel pit at Steinheim, near Stuttgart, in 1933

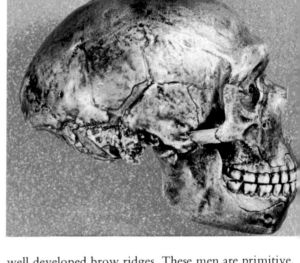

A Neanderthal skull: part of a nearly complete skeleton found in the limestone floor of a cave near the village of La Chapelle-aux-Saints, France

Casts of Neanderthal footprints preserved in the clay of an Italian cave floor

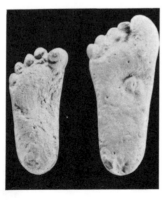

well developed brow ridges. These men are primitive, or archaic, *Homo sapiens*, though not so primitive as the Solo skulls of the same species, which may be slightly younger than the European finds.

Moving on to the last interglacial, the Eemian, which spans the period between about 70,000 and 100,000 years ago, several fossil men have been found in Europe. The few remains known indicate a fairly homogeneous neanderthaloid population from Italy (Saccopastore) to Germany (Ehringsdorf). In some ways these forms are a little more modern-looking than subsequent European Neanderthals; they have been called the 'early' or 'unspecialized' Neanderthals.

One puzzling set of specimens of this age from Fontéchevade in France has caused a great deal of argument. Parts of a skull cap are primitive and neanderthal; parts of the brow ridge and frontal are advanced and resemble modern man. Once again we have evidence of great variability – either within or between populations – in late Pleistocene time. The causes and meaning of this variability are unknown. (There is no reason to assume the Fontéchevade and Kanjera material belong to the same population!)

The original (those that were first described) or

'classic' Neanderthalers are known from Western Europe – Spain, France, Germany, Italy and Belgium – and seem to come from a fairly restricted time period, the early part of the last glaciation between 70,000 and about 50,000 years ago. The first adult Neanderthaler was recovered in 1856 from the Neander Valley near Dusseldorf in Germany; this material was known to Darwin. The classic Neanderthals as a group exhibit certain peculiar features. They have large brains (up to 1600 c.c.); large and inflated faces; long, low skulls with projecting occipitals and large brow ridges; long bones with massive joint surfaces; and large, powerful hands. They may be migrants from outside Europe but perhaps more probably they evolved in Europe from a pre-Würm stock. My own reconstruction of the Ehringsdorf skull (from the Eemian of Germany) makes it appear a great deal less modern and more classic Neanderthal than has been previously thought, and suggests that the Eemian men of Europe were not

An imaginatively reconstructed scene showing members of a Neanderthal family group near the Rock of Gibraltar about 75,000 years ago

so very different from classic Neanderthals. Much has been made of the 'ape-like' features of the Neanderthalers. In fact, their ape-like characters are non-existent. Their supposedly slouching gait was due to the inability of earlier workers to recognize the effects on the skeleton of arthritis! Neanderthal man stood and walked as we do.

In Europe Neanderthals of Eem and Würm age are associated with a complex of industries called the Mousterian. Mousterian industries are found in Eastern Europe, and the contiguous parts of Western Asia, southwestern Asia and North Africa. The Mousterian lasted in Western Europe until around 35,000 to 40,000 years ago, when it was replaced–apparently rather suddenly–by Upper Palaeolithic industries. These or related industries are also found outside Western Europe. In the Western regions the transition between Mousterian and Upper Palaeolithic industries is quite abrupt. Fossil men found associated with Upper Palaeolithic industries are similar to modern types. Hence it has been assumed that the break between the industries comes at the same time as a change in human populations, with modern types replacing the Neanderthalers. This traditional view has recently been challenged rather provocatively by Professor C. Loring Brace. As Brace points out, there is no definite evidence that the latest Mousterians in Western Europe were Neanderthals (the youngest of which are around 50,000 years old), nor that the oldest Upper Palaeolithics were *H. s. sapiens* (the oldest known of which in Western Europe being dubiously dated to around 30,000 years). He believes it possible for European Neanderthals to have evolved there into modern types. There probably was some population movement during this time even though the results may not have been quite so drastic as have been imagined. Actually, I think that altogether too much energy has been expended in arguments about Western Europe. Neither the hominids nor the stone tool industries there need necessarily be in any way typical of what was happening in other more important areas.

Mount Carmel man

Farther east in Europe and the adjacent parts of Asia
and Africa, populations similar to the Western Neanderthalers were living during early Würm times. They
differ from European men in certain minor ways, and
there is some evidence to suggest that local evolution
from earlier to modern man did occur in these areas.
Perhaps the most interesting area is southwestern Asia
and adjacent regions. In the later 1920s and early
1930s a large amount of skeletal material was recovered from Mount Carmel in Israel. The fossil
hominids come from two caves and are of two types.
The first group comes from Mugharet et Tabūn and is
archaic and resembles in some features the Western
European Neanderthals–particularly in the post-
cranial skeleton. Certain features of skull and teeth also
point to ties with Western Europe; however, other
characters link these hominids with those living at the
same time south of the Sahara in tropical Africa. The
Tabūn remains also resemble those from a cave near
Shanidar in Iraq. The Israel and Iraq hominids are
associated with a variety of the Mousterian industries.
I should repeat that they date from the early part of
the last glacial (70,000 to 50,000 years ago).

From exactly the same part of the world and, from
a similar time, come rather different remains. Hominids

*Site of the discovery of the Tabūn
remains on Mount Carmel, Israel*

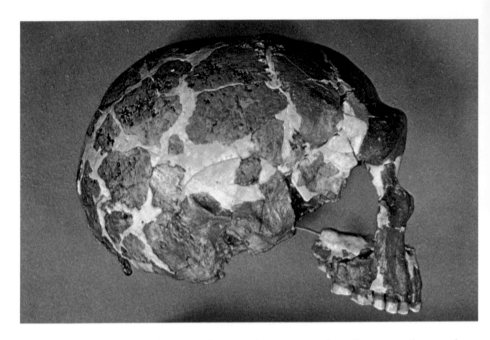

The extensively restored Tabūn skull, that of a Neanderthal woman about 30 years old, unearthed on Mount Carmel in 1931

with somewhat more modern features are known from Mugharet es-Skūhl on Mount Carmel, and from Djebel Kafzeh in Galilee. Cranially and post-cranially these men differ from the neanderthaloids of the same area, and they differ in a modern direction. Yet they are clearly related to the Neanderthaloids, and seem to represent at this time no more than different subspecies within a species. This population – or populations – probably represents the ancestors of modern *H. sapiens* in this particular area, as well as in Europe. I suspect that the as yet unknown ancestors of other, non-European, *H. s. sapiens* were living elsewhere in Africa, India and perhaps Asia, at the same time.

Fully modern skull-types first appear spasmodically in the fossil record about 50,000 or more years ago. After this, their frequency increases until whole populations and groups of populations are modern-looking. The reasons for the transformation and for the spread of modern types are as yet largely unknown. Another book would be needed to describe the origin and spread of *H. s. sapiens*, so complex is the story. A few

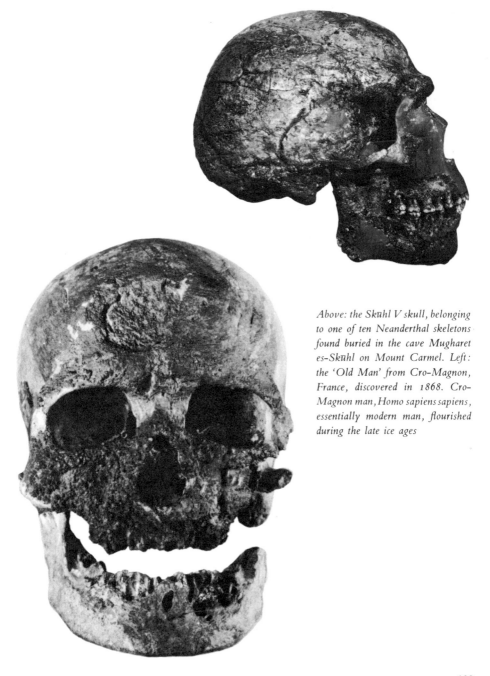

Above: the Skūhl V skull, belonging to one of ten Neanderthal skeletons found buried in the cave Mugharet es-Skūhl on Mount Carmel. Left: the 'Old Man' from Cro-Magnon, France, discovered in 1868. Cro-Magnon man, Homo sapiens sapiens, essentially modern man, flourished during the late ice ages

Early evidence of an elaborate human culture: the ornamented Grimaldi remains, in the Grotte des Enfants, Monaco, probably of a mother and her teen-age son

workers, Dr Leakey among them, believe that *H. erectus* and archaic subspecies of *H. sapiens* are side branches of human evolution and argue that the small, gracile, early Pleistocene hominids evolved directly into modern-looking men without passing through a heavy-skulled, big-browed phase. This argument is a little implausible mainly because of lack of supporting fossil evidence. It also appears unlikely that more than one species of man existed during the middle or late Pleistocene, so extensive would have been the ecological niche occupied by large-brained, cultural, tool-making hominids. Finally, the roundness and gracility of early Pleistocene skulls is probably due to their smallness and delicate construction and need imply no special relationship with *H. s. sapiens*.

Since the middle Pleistocene, the evidence points fairly firmly to the existence at any one time of just one species of hominid within the genus *Homo*. As successively younger fossils are examined, the morphology of hominids is seen to approach ever more closely that of ourselves; their stone tool cultures do likewise. We are dealing, then, with animals which are becoming more and more like us. During this entire time all men were living as hunter-gatherers. Only some 10,000 years ago were certain technological discoveries made which permitted the change to a settled, urban way of life which in turn brought with it great increases in population density, and the subsequent tremendous improvements (mostly in the last 100 years) in our technological prowess. Of course, these changes are all cultural changes, depending upon learned behaviour rather than upon any evolution of the brain. The detectable evolution of the brain and of genetically-determined behaviour, moulded by millions of years of hunting, tool-using behaviour ceased 50,000 or more years ago.

Hominids diverged from other primates well before the Pleistocene, probably sometime during the Miocene and at least 15 million years ago. Before this time the higher primates as a group had emerged from the prosimian level, and were living in complex, highly ordered social groups. Early on in their evolution the hominids became bipedal. Bipedalism would have been utilized both in the trees and on the ground in forest and woodland. Only in the Pliocene would hominids have ventured into the spreading savannahs. During this time, too, object manipulation and tool-use became ever more important and vital for hominid survival. The development of tool-using abilities, relatively unusual for primates, was probably part of a whole complex of alterations involving changes in food-getting behaviour (to hunting), and adjustments of social behaviour towards more cooperation and less aggressive interactions between troop members, particularly males. As tools replaced teeth as weapons, large male canines grew smaller, presumably to minimize the effects of any conflict within the group. Many other subtle psychological changes were also involved, all of them producing a primate no longer bounded by narrow territorial limits, but one that could use his new bipedalism and new tools to travel long distances in search of game.

Play behaviour in man and to a considerably lesser

extent in apes involves a great deal of object manipulation, far more than in any other primate. Now, play is of great importance to social mammals for in play the young practise the skills they will need in later life. A species learns easiest those skills which are adaptive; that is, those which are most useful to its particular way of life. These are the activities which are most pleasurable to it, which is why that species learns them. Object manipulation and tool-making come so easily to us because the hominid brain evolved to produce these particular, adaptively useful behaviours. It is interesting to note that the part of the human brain involved with neuromuscular control, the cerebellum, is particularly well developed in man, much more so than in apes. It may also have been slightly larger in *Australopithecus* than in the pongids.

The all-male groups found in many higher primates –chimps, geladas, some baboons–could easily develop into hunting bands, and the adoption of this new way of life required and induced many behavioural changes. First, truly cooperative behaviour must have appeared, as I have noted. Although this sort of behaviour is unusual in primates, animals that rarely cooperate in foraging for (mainly) vegetable food, it can be observed in social mammals like wolves and hunting dogs. Recent work on African social carnivores has shown that their behaviour and social structure is, like that of primates, extremely complicated. Food-sharing is prevalent among these carnivores, animals returning from the hunt and regurgitating food for those that have remained to protect pups and their nursing mothers.

Considerable interest has been directed towards social structure in these species because of the supposed parallels with the proto-human forms that first became cooperative hunters rather than solitary foragers. Kortlandt has attempted to list certain behavioural features which he believes would have characterized these early hominids. He notes the ease with which feelings of 'guilt' can be induced in dogs and wolves in cases where animals disobey (admittedly human) rules. He takes this to indicate that social carnivora possess rudimentary 'superegos' or 'consciences'. He then argues that it was the hunting way of life – the necessity for each animal to trust and rely on every other – that produced the complex of brain changes which would make all this possible. This is highly speculative of course, but still worth mentioning. Another possibly relevant point about social carnivore behaviour is that so-called pair-bonds – exclusive sexual relationships – are formed between an adult male and female, and these pairings may last for several years.

Human social behaviour

Let us assume that the social structure of the early hominids was roughly as follows: permanent pair-bonds would be the rule; males within a band would be sons, brothers or cousins, and their wives would be brought in from other groups in exchange for 'sisters'. In this way hunting bands consisting of males who trust one another can be formed, and the offspring have a permanent father to supply food and protection, as well as a permanent mother. I further assume that this kind of social structure evolved from something like that of the chimpanzee. That is, in which ties between mothers and offspring would be very strong and in which ties of friendship between male offspring may also be marked. It is unlikely that mating between mothers and sons occurs in chimps, and probably not between 'brothers' and 'sisters' either.

The first result of the adoption of hunting would have been a considerable sharpening in the division of labour between males and females, with the males doing the hunting while females were responsible for gathering vegetable food and taking care of the large-brained, relatively helpless, highly malleable hominid infant. It is possible, too, that permanent pair formation would also have evolved at about this time, each female having 'her' mate to provide for her while she could not do so herself. Kinship groups which previously consisted of mother and offspring would then increasingly include a biological father. This type of bonding was most probably an early feature of hominid evolution, important

A young woman, part Aborigine, photographed at Alice Springs, Australia, in 1896

because of its economic necessity. How might these ties have been built up, maintained and strengthened? Probably by sexual means.

The human type of sexual dimorphism is rather unusual in that males and females have canines of equal size and differ relatively little in body size—although males do tend to be a little larger and stronger. The human female also differs from her primate cousins in that she does not exhibit any oestrus cycle, the period of sexual receptivity occurring approximately every four weeks during which her behaviour, appearance and smell change, and during which males are actively solicited for purposes of copulation. Human females are sexually always receptive, the changes in behaviour springing from changes in the higher brain centres rather than hormonal cycles. The exact function of these alterations is not certainly known, but they can be interpreted as being associated with more or less permanent pair-bonding—the cementing of male-female ties. Year-round (or rather month-round) sexual behaviour encourages relatively permanent social bonds. The purpose of sexual behaviour seen in this light is to strengthen social ties, not just procreation. (This can be seen as yet another example of a general primate tendency to increase 'affectional' relationships.) With the alteration in type of receptivity from cyclical to continuous the fluctuating structural and behavioural changes in females have also gone, to be replaced—it has been suggested—by more permanent signals: prominent rounded breasts, exaggerated hips and buttocks, relatively hairless skin, and so on (surely not changes for the worse).

Other associated behavioural shifts occurring at the same time are too complex and too poorly understood to be listed here; but they would include the development of stealth, persistent and controlled motivation, curiosity, and further improvements in memory. Perhaps, too, the hominids had their first stirrings of 'conscience' or 'superego'. It is difficult to see how human society would have been possible without human conscience. Instead of having individuals con-

trolled by instincts, or even by the learned but geneti-
cally-channelled behaviour of the primate troop,
humans regulate their affairs by rules, customs, laws
and taboos. These can only work because we are
'designed' so that feelings of guilt can be induced in
situations where we have broken rules. Although
'conscience' and 'guilt' are not instinctive, we have
evolved a nervous system which makes it easy for this
guilt to be built up.

Aborigine father and son

As Dr Robin Fox has pointed out, one of the important areas in which guilt, or conscience, is important
is that of sexual behaviour within the family. So-called
'incest taboos' are those rules (not by any means universal) which forbid, with varying degrees of severity,
sexual relations between brothers and sisters, fathers
and daughters, and mothers and sons. In fact this last
relationship is about the only one which seems to be
constantly prohibited in human groups. Other, unlisted
(so to speak) relationships may also be forbidden; it
just depends on which relationships a particular society
decides are 'familial'. Probably the forbidden close

sexual relationships, those between mother and son and among offspring, are unlikely to have occurred anyway in our early ancestors. Only when 'father' was added to the family would father/daughter sex have to be prohibited, and it is interesting to note that this is the prohibition which is most frequently broken. Fox believes that incest taboos, for whatever reason their existence, are only possible because of the guilty feelings which can be induced about all sexual behaviour.

I must emphasize here the distinction between incest taboos, governing sexual behaviour, and marriage rules. Indeed it should be obvious to most western readers that sex and marriage often have little to do with each other! Human societies are universally characterized by incest taboos; all of them have marriage rules as well and most of these prohibit marriage between close relatives, the degree of allowable closeness being variable from culture to culture. Marriage as an institution was probably a somewhat later invention than either pair-bonding or incest taboos. It involves not just economic and sexual factors, but political factors as well. If 'marrying out' of the 'family' (however defined) is obligatory, then the nexus of kinship and political relationship between related bands can be spread over wide areas. This would have been very important for successful co-operative hunting on a large scale, and may only have developed at the late *Australopithecus africanus* stage.

It should be obvious that we are now well within the realms of human behaviour, and we can see what a complex of genetic determination and cultural learning it is. But none of this—incest taboos, pair-bonding, marriage rules, laws, perhaps even tool-making—would have been possible without the ability to name individuals, objects, and categories, and to externalize and describe previously internal feelings, ideas and concepts. In short, it would have been impossible without language. Although tool-making, and before that tool-using, have certainly been extremely important in human evolution, perhaps the most important behavioural feature differentiating man from other

Facial expressions as a means of communicating states of mind are almost as marked in chimpanzees as in humans. The face of the chimp below expresses attention. Those opposite are (top to bottom) a greeting pout, a smile, and a grimace of fear

primates, indeed from all other animals, is his possession
of vocal language.

Acquiring language

All primates produce sounds and many have a rich
vocal repertoire, as well as one of postures and gestures,
some of which may closely approximate those of man.
In primate species which have been really closely
studied it has been found that different alarm calls can
identify different predators and so signal differential
instructions to troop members. Information can also
be conveyed about food and water sources and about
the distribution of other animals. Most of the information transmitted by these vocalizations says something
about the internal, emotional state of the animal. We
too have a set of sounds to cover these sorts of situations.
'Ouch!', meaning 'the car door has a lot of static
electricity' is a good example of this sort of thing. However, these vocalizations do not do what language does.
They do not name, discuss, abstract or symbolize, but
human language does and thereby distinguishes us intel-
lectually from all other primates. Language is a tremendous aid to thinking, planning, memory, problem-
solving, cooperation, and many other activities. Once
established, at however rudimentary a level, selection
pressures would have acted very strongly to improve
and spread language capabilities. Certainly, to a hunting primate, one becoming organized socially along
proto-human lines, language would soon have become
indispensable.

In man the prodigious feat of language learning is
basically completed by the time infants are four or five
years old. The ease with which humans learn language
and the fact that the sequence of events in learning it
follows a standard pattern indicates that the ability to
learn language is built into the brain; not the ability to
learn any particular language, but to learn any sort of
language. Anthropologists and linguists have tried to
explain the evolution of language simply as one result
of our general intelligence, or because we stood erect
and rearranged the position of our larynx, thereby

permitting speech. Both explanations are unlikely. Baboons can make many of the sounds necessary for speech production; what they lack is central control in the brain.

Damage to many parts of the brain can affect speech production, showing that speech 'centres' are in fact quite widespread. Certain parts of the brain mature during the period in which language is acquired, and these areas mature independently of other systems (for example, of manipulative skills, locomotor behaviour, representational artistic ones, among others). Speech development in young children, whether English, Japanese, French or Russian, follows a regular pattern. After the one-word stage, they are able to organize two- and three-word 'sentences' in a regular, meaningful way, and in a manner which is not a degenerate imitation of adult speech. These word combinations are 'syntactical', they are structured and they convey meaning, and their existence implies that the human brain has built into it a propensity to organize words in a 'grammatical' way. Incidentally, these two- and three-word sentences show how an extremely rudimentary language could nevertheless convey a great deal of information. I am not saying that children are recapitulating in any way the evolution of language; merely pointing to a way in which very simple beginnings could have been made.

There is a certain peculiar type of human dwarf, known as a nanocephalic (or bird-headed) dwarf. These are perfectly proportioned but very diminutive persons whose brain volume may not exceed 300 or 400 c.c. In fact they have smaller brains with fewer functioning brain cells than many chimpanzees. Yet these people are capable of learning language and, although they are generally mentally defective, they behave in specifically human ways, not like apes! This clearly underlines the important point that it is brain structure rather than brain size which is so important in species-specific behaviour in general, and in this particular case of language. Just as our brains are built to manipulate objects, so too are we designed to acquire

A child learning to speak despite the handicap of congenital deafness

language and to learn it easily and with enjoyment.
These are our human species-specific behaviours and they are probably very ancient indeed. New pathways have been developed in the human brain which integrate visual, auditory, and tactile messages, permitting the sound of a particular (arbitrary) word to be 'connected to' any sort of object or idea, thus allowing the production of human speech. These areas, and those for word storage and so forth, are simply not present in other primates. Recently it has been reported that chimpanzees can be taught to attach non-verbal symbols to objects by using sign language; yet they are quite incapable of pairing sounds with these symbols. They do not have the right mental wiring.

Man the tool-maker

Anthropologists tend to favour the idea that truly human members of the genus *Homo* can be recognized by the first evidence for the *manufacture* of stone tools; tool-use is not enough. 'Tools' must be made to a set and regular pattern, and lately it has been argued that a 'tool' can only be acceptable if other tools are used in its manufacture. Of course, one can go on refining definitions like this indefinitely. Human evolution has certainly been marked by increasing reliance on objects external to the body; these behavioural changes form a continuum, like any evolving feature, and it is impossible to draw a non-arbitrary line through the continuum. Yet there is another point here. We hominids did not live by tools alone, and there is a great deal more to being human than just chipping a few flints. In contrast to other primates we can learn, plan, and cooperate in ways that would mystify even a chimpanzee. We can also control our emotions, our aggressions, our sexual drives, extremely well; and, finally, we can speak. Perhaps here lies the most important difference, yet one that is not detectable in the fossil record (although one might argue that the increasing standardization and improvement of tools might reflect increasing sophistication in linguistic communication). I believe that tool-making may simply indicate that widespread behavioural changes–associated with language evolution–had in fact already occurred. I should like to get away from too great an emphasis on tool-making, particularly in classifying hominids. For this reason I put *A. a. habilis* (or *A. habilis*) in *Australopithecus* and not automatically in *Homo*.

Although we have only very indirect evidence, it is obvious that 1 c.c. of hominid brain does not equal 1 c.c. of ape brain. We humans do not possess chimpanzee brains expanded three times. Although we do triple the ape volume, in fact we only have 25 per cent more brain cells (and the chimp itself has twice the number in a macaque brain). As well as structural changes in our brains, human brain cells are also different from those of apes: they are larger, more complex, with more interconnections. The chances are–even though this can never be proved–that *Australopithecus* brains were organized along basically human lines. (That is how they could evolve, finally, into humans!) *Australopithecus* was a biped, using arms and legs as we do; with dexterous, tool-making and weapon-using hands. As far as we can tell, *Australopithecus* differed in all manner of ways from apes–behaviourally, socially and anatomically. From *Australopithecus* on, there would have been changes in the richness and complexity of brain interconnections; improved language facility, symbolizing and learning ability; and improvements in memory, concentration, emotional control and so forth. These, however, would probably have been differences in degree only. That these changes were slow is evidenced by the slow rate of morphological and technological change throughout the early and middle Pleistocene, probably reflecting slow alterations in behaviour and brain structure. None the less, evolution did occur and brains became ever more efficient, until they reached 'take-off' point in the late Pleistocene. From Neolithic times onward, there were no more structural changes, only cultural ones.

It is natural, I think, to assume that our extra-large brains are linked to our undoubted intelligence; and there is a danger in thinking that brains are exclusively,

or even mainly, used in 'intellectual' pursuits. To quote
Dr S. M. Garn:

> It gratifies our ego to believe that selection favoured
> intelligence, that our own ancestral lines came to
> genetic fulfilment because they were so very smart.
> But it may be that our vaunted intelligence is merely
> an indirect product of the kind of brain that can dis-
> cern meaningful signals in a complex social context
> generating a heavy static of information or, rather,
> misinformational noise.

Here Garn is describing the brain as a kind of filter,
acting in a social context, sifting out what is important
from what is not. Most of us probably believe that the
natural property of minds is the manipulation of true
propositions, facts. But what if large brains evolved for
other reasons; what if our large brains are merely preadapted to be used for this kind of thinking? Here it is
appropriate to note what Professor Elman Service has
to say about the thinking of living hunter-gatherers:

> Even the amount of purely pragmatic information
> is bound to be limited simply because of the rudi-
> mentary technology of hunting-gathering societies.
> Another aspect of this is a lack of specialization;
> nobody is at work discovering things to be imparted
> at large for the good of the society. Perhaps this lack
> of specialization is the reason for the lack of abstrac-
> tion and generalization, as well as the absence of
> philosophizing about nature. It has often been asked,
> do primitive peoples understand cause-and-effect?
> In one sense they do, of course, as must anyone who
> has a normal contingent relationship to nature. But
> in an important sense primitive peoples do not seem
> to know the *principle* of cause-and-effect; it is not
> formulated as an abstraction. This is much like saying
> that although primitive persons must have some
> sense, for example, of geometrical relations, they do
> not have a geometry as such.

What sort of selection pressures might have caused
the increases in cell number, the changes in brain cells

and their interconnections, which resulted in brain expansion? We have Garn's suggestion, to which we could add the idea that an enlarging brain could be associated with improving language abilities. There is another, possibly complementary, explanation supplied by Professor G. E. Hutchinson. He notes, first, the tremendous complexity of human learned behaviour necessary for each of us to survive, and second, the fact that the most important human learning occurs during the first decade of life. This would include language acquisition, of course. Hutchinson suggests that big brains are 'adaptations to permit young individuals to learn how to behave in a population of individuals whose behaviour is unusually dependent on non-genetic information.'

In our own society, valued intellectual abilities like learning, insight, curiosity and imagination can be seen as extensions of juvenile attributes. (In a similar way mother-infant bonds in primate society were prototypes of adult affectional systems.) For most of hominid evolution adult behaviour has been conservative, acting as a suppressor mechanism preventing change. However, some cultures like ours have risked allowing individuals to extend these essentially juvenile intellectual capacities into adult life. We are only just glimpsing the full potential of the human intellect.

Adapting to the modern world

Yet, whatever happens in the future, human behaviour will always be channelled by certain factors. We can only behave, although admittedly with a high degree of flexibility, within the limits imposed by our 'natures'. After all, we are the product of millions of years of evolution as hunter-gatherers living in quite small groups. Within these groups, strong affectional feelings were directed towards a relatively small number of close relatives. Death, disaster, pain, unhappiness and numerous minor problems and misfortunes must have been common events to our ancestors, and too much time spent mourning or grieving would not have been good, efficient, adaptive behaviour. Similarly there would be numerous occasions on which men were faced with dangerous or stressful situations and to which they reacted with a whole array of nervous and hormonal responses ('fight or flight' reactions). Energy-yielding sugars and fats would be mobilized by the body to be utilized during these rapid and violent efforts.

Most human beings no longer live in hunting-gathering societies, but in overcrowded urban conditions with far higher population densities than were ever experienced by men of the stone age. We are faced with ever more stressful conditions, caused in part by sheer overcrowding, in part by what appears to be a steady breakdown in inter-personal relationships, and in part of course by our inability or unwillingness to control the steady pollution of our environment. We are constantly faced with stressful conditions to which we are not expected, or allowed, to react in the appropriate active or aggressive ways; and we are expected to project our positive feelings of warmth and friendship, reserved previously for close relatives and friends, towards people we may never even meet.

I am not suggesting that the very real problems of our society are due exclusively to these factors. What I am saying is that without a real understanding of our structural and behavioural evolution, without a full knowledge of our closest relatives, in fact without understanding ourselves past and present, we cannot hope to face the problems of the future with any hope of success. No academic worker needs to justify his work in any terms other than sheer personal exhilaration and enjoyment; but I believe that a combined biological and cultural approach to human evolution, as I understand it the major subject matter of physical anthropology, has an indispensable part to play in assuring a successful collective human future.

GLOSSARY

advanced: term applied to characteristics occurring later in a lineage, or similar to those occurring later in evolution.

analogy: similarity due not to inheritance from a common ancestor but to similar function.

Anthropoidea (higher primates): taxon containing all non-prosimian primates: monkeys, apes, and men.

ape: the four living Old World apes of the zoological family Pongidae are the gibbon, gorilla, chimpanzee, and orang utan. All, unlike the monkeys, lack tails.

arboreal: tree-dwelling.

brachiation: form of locomotion in which the arms alone are used to move the body forward.

Calabrian: period of time beginning about $1\frac{3}{4}$ million years ago; name used originally in southern Italy for marine rocks laid down after that time and before the large-scale continental glaciations.

canine: projecting tusk-like teeth, particularly large in male primates. In man they have become greatly reduced in size and changed in shape, although even today human canines may be pointed.

capitate: small wrist bone.

Catarrhine: taxon of Anthropoidea including the Old World monkeys, apes, and man; evolved originally in Africa.

Cretaceous: period of geological time ending about 65 million years ago.

culture: those aspects of human behaviour – rituals, myths, laws, religion, etc – which are learned and transmitted from one generation to another by learning.

cusp: protuberance on the chewing surface of a tooth.

dentition: the teeth.

ecological: of the relationship of plants and animals to their environment.

environment: surrounding objects or circumstances, animate or inanimate, which may affect an animal's or plant's life; includes other animals or plants of the same species.

Eocene: period between 56 and 37 million years ago.

femur: thigh bone.

fibula: the outer of the two shank bones.

foramen magnum: hole in the base of the skull through which the spinal cord passes.

heteromorphic: having the front lower premolar a single-cusped sectorial, cutting, tooth and the rear lower premolar a bicuspid tooth.

hominid: member of the zoological family Hominidae, containing living and fossil men and their ancestors.

homology: similarity due to inheritance from a common ancestor.

homomorphic: having both front and rear lower premolars of the same bicuspid form.

incisors: chisel-shaped teeth at the front of the jaw.

knuckle-walker: the chimpanzee and gorilla; quadrupeds that habitually support their weight on the backs of the middle parts of their flexed fingers.

lineage: ancestral-descendant series of populations through time at any level up to that of species.

Miocene: period of geological time between 26 and 12 million years ago.

molars: multi-cusped teeth at the rear of the jaw.

monkey: higher primates with tails: New World monkeys (Platyrrhini) and Old World monkeys (Catarrhini).

morphological: pertaining to form or structure.

morphospecies: species described wholly in terms of morphological characteristics.

niche: particular part of the environment which a species exploits and utilises.

occipital: rear part of head region.

Oligocene: period of geological time between 37 and 26 million years ago.

Palaeocene: period of geological time between 65 and 56 million years ago.

parallelism: similarities arising in separate but related evolutionary lines due to similar selective factors.

Platyrrhini: taxon of Anthropoidea including the New World monkeys, a group which evolved in Central and South America.

Pleistocene: period of geological time between 2 million years ago and the present day.

Pliocene: period of geological time between 12 and 2 million years ago.

pongid: member of the zoological family Pongidae, containing living apes and their ancestors and relatives.

premolar: teeth between canines and molars; generally bicuspid.

Primates: zoological order to which man, apes, monkeys, and prosimians belong, together with their extinct ancestors and relatives.

primitive: term applied to characteristics occurring earlier in a lineage, or similar to those occurring earlier in evolution.

Prosimii: group to which certain primitive primates—lemurs, bush-babies, tarsiers—belong, together with their extinct ancestors and relatives.

species: biological: largest naturally occurring group of animals or plants capable of interbreeding with the production of fully fertile offspring. Evolutionary or time-successive species: group of ancestral-descendant biological species populations evolving through time from an arbitrary beginning to an arbitrary end. (See 'morphospecies'.)

talus: uppermost of the tarsal bones connecting foot to leg.

tarsus: small bones of the foot.

taxon: group of individuals or species at any level of hierarchic classification.

taxonomist: scientist who classifies plants or animals.

tibia: inner of the two shank bones.

vertical clinging and leaping: type of posture and locomotion in which animal normally rests clinging to a vertical support, leaps by pushing off with powerful hind-limbs, and lands feet first on a vertical support.

Villafranchian: period of time beginning about $3\frac{1}{2}$ million years ago; name used originally in Europe for rocks laid down on the land (rather than in the sea) after that time and before the large-scale continental glaciations.

BIBLIOGRAPHY

1 Evolution and Man

Carter, G. S., *A Hundred Years of Evolution.* London 1957.

Darwin, Charles, *The Origin of Species.* London, 1859.

— *The Descent of Man, and Selection in Relation to Sex.* London, 1871.

De Beer, G., *Charles Darwin: A Scientific Biography.* New York, 1964.

Pilbeam, D. R., 'Human Origins.' *Advancement of Science*, March 1968.

2 The Substance of Evolution

Dobzhansky, Th., *Mankind Evolving: The Evolution of the Human Species.* Yale, 1962.

Mayr, Ernst, *Animal Species and Evolution.* Harvard, 1963.

Simpson, G. G., *The Major Features of Evolution.* New York, 1953.

— *Principles of Animal Taxonomy.* New York, 1961.

3 The Primates

DeVore, Irven (ed.), *Primate Behavior: Field Studies of Monkeys and Apes.* New York, 1965.

Jay, P. C. (ed.), *Primates: Studies in Adaptation and Variability.* New York, 1968.

Napier, J. R., and P. H., *A Handbook of Living Primates.* London, 1967.

Pilbeam, D. R., 'Man's Earliest Ancestors.' *Science Journal*, February 1967.

Reynolds, Vernon, 'Open Groups in Hominid Evolution.' *Man*, Vol. I 441–52 (1966).

— *The Apes: The Gorilla, Chimpanzee, Orangutan and Gibbon – Their History and Their World.* London 1967.

Simons, E. L., 'The Earliest Apes.' *Scientific American*, December 1967.

4 Man's Unique Features

Buettner-Janusch, John, *Origins of Man.* New York, 1966.

Campbell, B. G., *Human Evolution: An Introduction to Man's Adaptations.* Chicago, 1966

Howells, William, *Mankind in the Making.* London, 1967.

Le Gros Clark, W. E., *The Antecedents of Man: An Introduction to the Evolution of the Primates.* Edinburgh, 1959.

— *The Fossil Evidence for Human Evolution: An Introduction to the Study of Paleoanthropology.* Chicago, 1964.

Napier, John, 'The Antiquity of Human Walking.' *Scientific American*, April, 1967.

5 Man's Earliest Ancestors

Pilbeam, David, 'Notes on *Ramapithecus,* the Earliest Known Hominid, and *Dryopithecus.*' *American Journal of Physical Anthropology*, n.s. 25, 1–5 (1966).

Simons, E. L., 'The Early Relatives of Man.' *Scientific American*, July, 1964.

Straus, W. L. Jr., 'The Classification of Oreopithecus.' In Washburn, S.L. (ed.) *Classification and Human Evolution.* Wenner-Gren Foundation, Viking Fund Publication 37, 146–177 (1963).

6 The Ice-Age Epoch

Cox, A., Dalrymple, A. B. and Doell, R. R., 'Removals of Earth's Magnetic Field.' *Scientific American*, February 1967.

Emiliani, Cesare, 'The Pleistocene Epoch and the Evolution of Man.' *Current Anthropology* 9, 27–47 (1968).

Flint, R. F. *Glacial and Pleistocene Geology.* New York, 1957.

Glass, B., Ericson, D. B., Heezen, B. C., Opdyke, N. D., and Glass, J. A. 'Geomagnetic Reversals and Pleistocene Chronology.' *Nature* 216, 437–42 (1967).

7 The Earliest Men

Howell, F. C., *Early Man,* New York, 1965.

Le Gros Clark, W. E., *Man-apes or Ape-men?* Chicago, 1965.

Pilbeam, D. R. and Simons, E. L., 'Some Problems of Hominid Classifications.' *American Scientist* 53, 237–259.

Weiner, J. S., *The Piltdown Forgery*. London, 1955.

8 Man's Recent Ancestors

Brace, C. L., 'The Fate of the "Classic" Neanderthals: A Consideration of Hominid Catastrophism.' *Current Anthropology* 5, 3–43 (1964).

Coon, C. S., *The Origin of Races*. London, 1962.

Howell, F. C., 'Pleistocene Glacial Ecology and the Evolution of "Classic Neanderthal" Man.' *Southwestern Journal of Anthropology* 8, 377–410 (1952).

Howells, W. W., 'Homo erectus.' *Scientific American*, November 1966.

Oakley, K. P., *Man the Tool-Maker*. London, 1961.

9 Human Behavioural Evolution

Fox, Robin, *Kinship and Marriage*. London, 1967.

Geschwind, N., 'The Development of the Brain and the Evolution of Language.' In C.I.J.M. Stuart (ed.), *Rept. 15th Annual Round Table Meeting on Linguistics and Language Studies*. Monograph Series in Language and Linguistics No. 17, Georgetown University Press.

Holloway, R. L. Jr., 'Tools and Teeth: Some Speculations Regarding Canine Reduction.' *American Anthropologist* 69, 63–67 (1967).

Lee, R. B. and DeVore, Irven (eds.), *Man the Hunter*. Chicago, 1968.

Lenneberg, E. H. (ed.), New Direction in the Study of Languages. Cambridge, Mass., 1964.

Service, E. R., *The Hunters*. New Jersey, 1966.

SOURCES OF ILLUSTRATIONS

INDEX